ONE HUNDRED SPEECHES FROM THE THEATER

ONE HUNDRED SPEECHES FROM THE THEATER

Selected by Rona Laurie

FOREWORD BY BARBARA VANN

CROWELL-COLLIER PRESS
Division of Macmillan Publishing Co., Inc.
New York

Originally published in Great Britain by Evans Brothers Ltd.
Twelve selections in the English edition were
replaced by speeches specially chosen for the American edition.
Copyright © 1966 Rona Laurie
Copyright © 1973 Macmillan Publishing Co., Inc.
Macmillan Publishing Co., Inc.,
866 Third Avenue, New York, N.Y. 10022
Library of Congress catalog card number: 72-81070
Printed in the United States of America
10   9   8   7   6   5   4   3   2   1

The acknowledgments on pages 187 through 192 constitute an
extension of this copyright page.

Library of Congress Cataloging in Publication Data

Laurie, Rona, ed.
One hundred speeches from the theater.

London ed. published in 1966 under title: A hundred
speeches from the theatre.
"Twelve selections in the English edition were replaced by
speeches specially chosen for the American edition."
1. Drama—Collections. [1. Plays—Collections]
I. Title.
PN6112.L282   808.82   72-81070   ISBN 0-02-754610-1

FOREWORD

The material offered in this book should both dismay and delight the young actor. Dismay (although not irrevocably) because the variety and scope of speeches call for a command of style and technique that means hours of hard and fundamental work. One method will not satisfy all types of writing. The actor must be able to sink into psychological problems, focus upon the world through another's eyes, play with language and tricks of reality and illusion, and choose which approach fits which material. This last factor can be learned only through experience and the actor's personal discovery of his own resources and what stimulates them. Then he must train his "instrument," his voice, his body, his perceptions. He must lend himself to his art in a complete and unselfish manner. If he does not, art becomes chicanery.

The realm of delight is a complex one. This book is, not surprisingly, a collection of words. The very volume of them is awesome. One thinks of myriad playwrights churning out words and sentences and scenes (and here comes the delight) for the actor to transform into a living event. The scenes have meaning, of course, but they also function as a means of transport between the actor and the audience. The actor makes live theater happen—he acts to fill a room with a community of the present. The audience has made its step. It has come to the place. It is more or less available, vulnerable.

In a classroom situation the same connection is present. The tempo may be slower, the audience more indulgent, or at any rate looking for different values, but the process is the same. It is to be noted that few of the selected scenes are monologues, in the sense that the actor is alone on the stage. Most call for the participation of characters other than the one with the "speech." The actor would be wise to make use of another person to whom to relate. Few events of any interest exist in a vacuum, and a character gains definition and dimension in relation, or in opposition, to another. Add the audience, and the interplay can lift the scene to another level of experience.

Within the rigorous framework of a written piece a minor miracle may occur. Once an actor has experienced the delight of opening out into a live moment, of filling a room with a current of excitement, the labor and disappointments of the craft fade away. Then the circle is complete, for he will return to his training with a renewed desire to improve this craftsmanship, to allow himself even greater freedom fully to "act" upon the stage.

BARBARA VANN

PREFACE

This book contains a challenge to every actor and to every would-be actor. Each speech has been chosen because it is a dramatically effective piece of writing, but it is the actor's job to lift the playwright's words off the printed page and to give them life and dramatic impact. The performance of an isolated speech involves a special technique and the actor's approach to it will be different from his approach if he were acting the part in its entirety. Then he has time to build up his character gradually—a stroke here, a highlight there—so that we may not get the complete picture of the character until the final curtain. In a single speech, however, the quintessence of the character must be realized and suggested in the performance although perhaps only one aspect of the part is emphasized in those particular lines. Therefore, it is essential that the whole play be studied carefully before the actor begins to work on the excerpt.

Great concentration is called for before the first word is spoken. The actor has to visualize the situation in the play at the point where the speech occurs and to know what stage of development the character has reached at that moment. This will obviously affect timing, movement and the emotional temperature of the speech.

Again, the performance of an isolated speech involves a special technique in that the actor has to engage the interest of his audience from the very first line—he has no time to "play himself in." He has to achieve dramatic shape within the speech and an ending that is something more than the cessation of the voice. Economy is called for if the maximum effect is to be made. This involves the actor's judgment and powers of selection, for the speech must not be given more weight than its structure will bear, just as it is useless to try to pour a pint into a half-pint tankard.

And then there is the question of style. Many of the excerpts in this book have been written by today's playwrights but no attempt has been made to restrict the choice to one period or to one trend in the theater. Thus *Everyman* will be found cheek by jowl with *The Caretaker* and The Wakefield Mystery Plays with those of Arnold Wesker. Each one demands a different approach and poses different problems for the actor. As far as possible, excerpts have been chosen that are self-explanatory, but occasionally it may be felt that a few words of introduction to put the audience in the picture are necessary. To this end, and also as an aid to study, brief notes have been given before each speech.

Finally, my aim has been to pack the book with the stuff of live theater which, as Sir Tyrone Guthrie says in *A Life in the Theatre* (McGraw-Hill), "will survive all threats from powerfully organized industries which pump prefabricated drama out of cans and blowers and contraptions of one kind or another. The struggle for survival may often be hard and will batter the old theater about severely. Indeed, from time to time it will hardly be recognizable; but it will survive. It will survive as long as mankind demands to be amused, terrified, instructed, shocked, corrupted and delighted by tales told in the manner which will always remain mankind's most vivid and powerful manner, of telling a story. I believe that the purpose of the theater is to show mankind to himself, and thereby to show to man God's image."

RONA LAURIE

CONTENTS

PART TWO ❖ SPEECHES FOR MEN
DRAMATIC SPEECHES

CHARACTER AND DIALECT

* Selection and headnote by Barbara Vann

Part One

SPEECHES
FOR WOMEN

DRAMATIC SPEECHES

CAMINO REAL
Tennessee Williams

Marguerite Gautier, the famous "Lady of the Camellias," is described by Tennessee Williams as a beautiful woman of indefinite age. In this speech she is talking to another of the legendary figures in the play—Jacques Casanova. The play is set outside of time in a place of no specific locality, in a kind of limbo where the characters wait before moving on to an unknown future. Marguerite says: "This is a port of entry and departure, there are no permanent guests!" The speech is rhythmical; her words are suffused with sadness and with nostalgia for her past life and tenderness for Jacques, caught, like her, in this "dim, shadowy end of the Camino Real."

BLOCK 10

MARGUERITE: Oh, Jacques, we're used to each other, we're a pair of captive hawks caught in the same cage, and so we've grown used to each other. That's what passes for love at this dim, shadowy end of the Camino Real. . . .

What are we sure of? Not even of our existence, dear comforting friend! And whom can we ask the questions that torment us? "What is this place? Where are we?"—a fat old man who gives sly hints that only bewilder us more, a fake of a gypsy squinting at cards and tea leaves. What else are we offered? The never-broken procession of little events that

3

assure us that we and strangers about us are still going on! Where? Why? and the perch that we hold is unstable!

We're threatened with eviction, for this is a port of entry and departure, there are no permanent guests! And where else have we to go when we leave here? Bide-a-While? "Ritz Men Only"? Or under that ominous arch into Terra Incognita? We're lonely. We're frightened.

We hear the streetcleaners' piping not far away. So now and then, although we've wounded each other time and again— we stretch out hands to each other in the dark that we can't escape from—we huddle together for some dim communal comfort—and that's what passes for love on this terminal stretch of the road that used to be royal. What is it, this feeling between us? When you feel my exhausted weight against your shoulder—when I clasp your anxious old hawk's head to my breast, what is it we feel in whatever is left of our hearts? Something, yes, something—delicate, unreal, bloodless! The sort of violets that could grow on the moon, or in the crevices of those faraway mountains, fertilized by the droppings of carrion birds. Those birds are familiar to us. Their shadows inhabit the plaza. I've heard them flapping their wings like old charwomen beating worn-out carpets with gray brooms. . . . But tenderness, the violets in the mountains—can't break the rocks!

COLOMBE

Jean Anouilh, *translated by D. Cannan*

The play is set in a theater in Paris in 1900. Colombe and Julien have been married for two years. Julien is hoping to become a concert pianist but his career has been interrupted by his military service. He has been away for three months and in this scene he returns to find that Colombe, encouraged by his mother, a famous actress, has taken to the life of the theater like a duck to water. Colombe tells him that everything is finished between them. She is now more interested in his brother, Paul. Julien has been jealous and possessive during their brief married life and Colombe's butterfly nature has been released while he has been away. She is young, fresh, radiant and loves life, but she has now become a more brittle character than she is in the earlier part of the play. Although written in prose, this speech has poetic quality.

ACT III

COLOMBE: Now, I can live for myself. I only began to be happy the day after you'd gone. I woke up, the sun was shining, I drew back the curtains and for the first time there was nothing but happiness in the street. The baker's boy whistled when he saw me at the window, and I smiled and said "Good morning," and there was no one to blame me all the rest of the day, because I'd answered him. And if the postman rang the bell before I was up, there was no one to tell me I was a fallen woman if I opened the door in my nightdress. He was a happier postman for seeing a pretty girl in her nightie, and I was a happier girl in seeing that it gave him pleasure. I cleaned the rooms as if it were a game, and I put a basin of water in the sunshine and stood in it naked, to wash myself—and what did it matter if the old man opposite was getting a treat through his binoculars? It was a natural joy to both of us, a present from God as much as the sun on the trees.

5

THE DEVILS

John Whiting

The play is set in and near Loudon between the years 1623 and 1634. Sister Jeanne, a humpback, now Mother of the Convent, has invited Grandier, the priest, to become the Director of the House. After his refusal Jeanne believes that she is possessed by visions of a diabolical nature and that an evil spirit has gained entry to her through Grandier. In this scene, which takes place in the Convent garden, Jeanne is trying to explain to some of the Sisters what has happened. Sister Louise has asked her: "What shall we do, Mother? People are taking their children away from us," and "Have we mocked God?" This speech is Sister Jeanne's reply.

ACT II

JEANNE: It was not the intention.

But to make a mockery of man. That's a different matter! For what a splendid creature he makes to be fooled. He might have been created for no other purpose. With his head in the air, besotted with his own achievement, he asks to be tripped. Deep in the invention of mumbo-jumbo to justify his existence, he is deaf to laughter. With no eyes for anything but himself, he's blind to the gesture of ridicule made in front of his face.

So, drunk, deaf and blind, he goes on. The perfect subject for the practical joke. And that, my sisters, is where the children of misfortune—like me—play a part. We do not mock our beloved Father in Heaven. Our laughter is kept for His wretched and sinful children who get above their station, and come to believe they have some other purpose in this world than to die.

After the delusions of power come the delusions of love. When men cannot destroy they start to believe they can be saved by creeping into a fellow human being. And so per-

6

petuating themselves. Love me, they say over and over again, love me. Cherish me. Defend me. Save me. They say it to their wives, their whores, their children, and some to the whole human race. Never to God. These are probably the most ridiculous of all, and most worthy of derision. For they do not understand the glory of mortality, the purpose of man: loneliness and death.

Let us go in.

THE HOLLY
AND THE IVY
Wynyard Browne

Margaret, a clergyman's daughter, has been living with Robert, an American who has been killed. Their child, Simon, has died of meningitis at the age of four. Now, a year after this second tragedy, Margaret, bitter and disillusioned, has come back to the vicarage. Her family has known nothing of her life in London. Here she is talking to her father for the first time about what has happened during the years in which she has been away.

ACT III

MARGARET: Listen. Robert was killed—I really did love him, you know—and after that I found I was going to have Simon. That seemed important. Not only because of Robert, but because, well . . . another life in the world is important. And so, for the next four years, of course, I did everything I possibly could for Simon. Then—he died. And I just felt—what was the point of it all? What was the value of all that effort? Don't you see? It was then that I first began to realize that, in the long run, it's the same for everyone. Practically all the efforts that people make are simply to keep life going— their own or someone else's. And the whole thing's doomed to failure. We know that. Life can't be kept going indefinitely. The sun's growing cold and, in the end, the human race it- self'll be frozen off the earth. What sense does that make? Oh, I know what you'll say—about immortality and so on. But I just can't believe that. And even if I could, that's not quite the point. I'm not just sentimentally unhappy because I shan't see Bob and Simon again. I'm not the type that starts going to séances because someone I love is dead. That's not the point. I want to be sure that all the values we try to establish are real values. I want to relate life, here and now, not only my own life, but all life, to whatever may be true about the universe.

THE LARK

Jean Anouilh, *translated by Christopher Fry*

In this scene Joan of Arc withdraws the admission of guilt forced out of her in her captivity. She is talking to Beauchamp, earl of Warwick. Throughout his play, Anouilh puts the em- phasis on the ultimate happiness of Joan's story when, freed by the fire, she soars above the conflict of church and state. Joan's practical, earthy side has to be conveyed as well as her spiritu- ality. It would be interesting for the actress to compare the parallel scene in Shaw's *Saint Joan*.

PART II

JOAN: But I don't want things to adjust themselves. I don't want to live through however long this "in time" of yours will be. (*She gets up like a sleepwalker, and stares blindly ahead*) Do you see Joan after living through it, when things have adjusted themselves: Joan, set free, perhaps, and vegetating at the French Court on her small pension? (*Almost laughing, though sadly*) Joan accepting everything, Joan fat and complacent, Joan doing nothing but eat. Can you see me painted and powdered, trying to look fashionable, getting entangled in her skirts, fussing over her little dog, or trailing a man at her heels: who knows, perhaps with a husband?

(*Suddenly cries out in another voice*) But I don't want everything to come to an end! Or at least not an end like that, an end which is no end at all. Blessed St. Michael: St. Margaret: St. Catherine! You may be silent now, but I wasn't born until you first spoke to me, that day in the fields: my life truly began when I did what you told me to do, riding horse-back with a sword in my hand. And that is Joan, and no other one. Certainly not one sitting placid in her convent, pasty-faced and going to pieces in comfort: continuing to live as a tolerable habit: set free, they would call it! You kept yourself silent, God, while all the priests were trying to speak at once, and everything became a confusion of words. But You told St. Michael to make it clear to me in the very beginning, that when You're silent You have then the most certain trust in us. It is the time when You let us take on everything alone. (*She draws herself up*) Well, I take it on, O God: I take it upon myself! I give Joan back to You: true to what she is, now and forever! Call your soldiers, Warwick; call them, call them, quickly now: for I tell you I withdraw my admission of guilt: I take back my promises: they can pile their faggots, and set up their stake: they can have their holiday after all.

9

You have to have courage, that's all; I shall have courage. (*She looks at his pale face and puts a hand on his shoulder*) You're a good, dear fellow, in spite of your gentlemanly poker face; but there isn't anything you can do: we belong, as you say, to different ways of life. (*She unexpectedly gives him a little kiss on the cheek, and runs off, calling*) Soldiers, goddams! Hey there, goddams! Fetch me the clothes I wore to fight in, and when I'm back in my breeches tell all my judges Joan is herself again!

MISS JULIE

August Strindberg, *translated by Michael Meyer*

This one-act play is set in South Sweden during the 1880s. Miss Julie is twenty-five and here she is talking to her father's valet, Jean. She has just become his mistress. The actress has to convey Julie's feverish vitality.

MISS JULIE: You're only saying that. Anyway, everyone else knows. You see, my mother was a commoner, of quite humble birth. She was brought up with ideas about equality, freedom for women and all that. And she had a decided aversion to marriage. So when my father proposed to her, she replied that she would never become his wife, but—well, anyway, she did. I came into the world, against my mother's wish as far as I can gather. She wanted to bring me up as a child of nature, and into the bargain I was to learn every-

thing that a boy has to learn, so that I might stand as an example of how a woman can be as good as a man. I had to wear boy's clothes, and learn to look after horses—though I was never allowed to enter the cowshed. I had to groom and saddle them, and hunt—I even had to try to learn about agriculture. Meanwhile, on the estate, all the men were set to perform the women's tasks, and the women the men's—with the result that it began to do badly, and we became the laughingstock of the district. In the end my father came to his senses and put his foot down, and everything was changed back to the way he wanted it. My mother fell ill—what illness, I don't know—but she often had convulsions, hid herself in the attic and the garden, and sometimes stayed out all night. Then there was the great fire which you have heard about. The house, the stables and the cowshed were all burned down, under circumstances suggesting arson—for the accident happened the very day our quarterly insurance had expired, and the premium my father sent had been delayed through the inefficiency of the servant carrying it, so that it hadn't arrived in time. (*Fills her glass and drinks*)
JEAN: Don't drink any more.
MISS JULIE: Oh, what does it matter? So we were left penniless, and had to sleep in the carriages. My father couldn't think where he would be able to find the money to rebuild the house. Then mother advised him to ask for a loan from an old friend of hers, a brick merchant who lived in the neighborhood. Father got the money free of interest, which rather surprised him. So the house was rebuilt. (*Drinks again*) Do you know who burned the house down?

Omit Jean's line.

THE QUEEN AND THE REBELS

Ugo Betti, *translated by Henry Reed*

The play is set in a room on an unlocalized frontier. Argia, a
peasant, has been mistaken for the real queen of the country,
who is fleeing from the rebels. Argia is a slut, but when the
situation arises she finds the spiritual strength to play the part
of a queen with conviction and dignity. For the first time in
her life she feels herself free to make decisions, and at the end
of the play she faces her death with courage. Here she is speaking to Amos, one of the revolutionaries.

ACT IV

ARGIA (*her teeth chattering*): What you're saying, in fact,
is that if there were here, in my place, some less fortunate
woman than I, someone who'd had to cook herself an egg
in her room, you're saying that there'd be some real merit
in *her,* if she were courageous at this moment? Commissar
Amos, there was once a woman whom they played a joke on.
I was told about it. One Sunday, this woman went to the
seaside. And the bathing attendants, for a joke, knowing the
sort of woman she was, got out for her a bathing costume of
the kind that becomes almost transparent in the water. There
was a good deal of merriment. And all of a sudden, the
woman noticed that everyone was looking at her, and there
was rather a row going on.

AMOS: Come on; the names.

ARGIA: And at last that woman saw that she was standing
there almost naked! Alone and naked. She stood there be-
wildered. And suddenly, do you know what she did? She
tried to laugh, with them. (*Controlling herself, and shrug-
ging her shoulders*) And after all what did they see? That she
was a woman. We know what a woman is. A man comes up
to her . . . cheerful, with his big, sweaty hands, and says,

12

"Do this . . . go like this . . . do that . . . (*louder*) . . . go on . . . ." (*Suddenly, with a real cry of anguish and protest*) Well, do you know what I think! I think there comes a time when the only thing to do is to stand up and say . . . (*as though actually turning on someone*) "Why do you insult me like this? And, my God, why have I allowed you to? Get away from me! Go away! Go away! Leave me alone! You take advantage of an immense mistake, a monstrous delusion! Respect me! Show me respect! Respect . . . because I am . . . the Queen! The Queen, and destined for other things than this." (*With a change of voice*) What I want to do is to go out of doors, as if it were a fine morning, and as if I had seen down there, at the end of the street, the cool fresh color of the sea, a color that makes the heart leap! And someone stops me, and then someone else, and someone else, with the usual rudenesses. But this morning I don't even hear them. I'm not afraid any longer. My face expresses dignity. I am as I would always have wished to be.

Omit Amos's line.

A QUESTION OF FACT

Wynyard Browne

The playwright, Wynyard Browne, has said that this is a play about imagination and that only by imagination can we grasp the truth about our fellow men. But the imagination must be used with love.

Rachael is an ordinary girl caught in an extraordinary situation. Her husband, Paul, is the son of a murderer. Rachel has only just discovered this. Because she truly loves Paul she is able to find the right words as she tries to explain to him the nature of love.

ACT III

RACHEL: But . . . I don't want to escape . . . I love you. You're not, you're not like your father. Loving you would become misery, anxiety, terror. . . . As it is becoming already. You don't think I'm happy, do you? I've never been happy for more than a day or two since we married. You've never given me a chance. . . . Oh, yes it can make that sort of difference—the difference between happiness and misery—but it can't make the difference between loving you and not loving you. Nothing can do that . . . ever.

Oh, God! I can't stand this! Love, I'm talking about, love, love, love! Not esteem, not respect, not something you can earn by good conduct or lose by bad behavior. Love isn't rational. It's something that *happens* . . . I don't love you for your sake, out of kindness, but for my own. . . . No, it's not even that. I love you whether I like it or not, however much harm it does me. . . . Even when you're aloof, ironic, frightening even—yes, even then—don't you understand? My heart turns over with love for you because of the way you laugh, or move your hands. . . . For better, for worse . . . that's not a vow, it's a description.

14

THE REHEARSAL

Jean Anouilh, *translated by*
Pamela Hansford Johnson and Kitty Black

The setting of this play—one of Anouilh's *pièces brillantes*—
is an eighteenth-century castle. The count and the guests in his
house party are rehearsing a play by Marivaux; they are dressed
in eighteenth-century costume. The count falls in love with
Lucile, a young nursemaid whom he has invited to take part in
the play.

The countess is a beautiful, intellectual and poised woman of
the world. Although no emotional depths are plumbed here, the
actress should convey some warmth and charm. She is talking
to Lucile in this speech.

ACT II

COUNTESS: You know, I like you a great deal. . . . You're
really so young, so defenseless with your little air of knowing
everything. I'm sure that under all that high-mindedness,
you're more than ready to burn your wings like a delicate
insect at the first candle that comes your way. You say to
yourself, won't it be beautiful! At last it will be the life I've
always dreamed about. . . . For a week you live in that
dream, and afterward, you're left with only your eyes to weep
with. Damien told me you were proud and poor. That's a
great virtue, with a very great defect. When a girl's fastidious,
pretty, clever and penniless, she's always a little *déclassée*.
Think it over. I can speak to you as a woman who knows
what life is, who is very much older than you are, and who
would be miserable—really miserable—to see you throwing
away your beautiful youth for some folly with no future to it.
When a girl is alone in the world, her first thought must be
for the future. Heavens! I know it can't be much fun—at
twenty, one has all sorts of other dreams—but that's the way
the world goes, my dear. We can do nothing about it.

15

THE TIGER AND THE HORSE
Robert Bolt

Mrs. Dean, the wife of the Master of the College, is about fifty-four years old; Robert Bolt describes her in these words: "Her movements are healthy and vigorous; she is the nut-brown maid. But a mass of meaningless lines runs about her face, her large clear eyes are frightened." At this point in the play she has become mentally unbalanced and has slashed a valuable picture with her gardening shears. Here she is trying to explain to her husband, Jack, the fact that they have "never, never in anything been together." The stage directions provide valuable guidance to the actress.

ACT III

MRS. DEAN: Don't, Jack! I know it's kindly meant, dear, but it serves no further purpose and it hurts. Why, it was *you* who showed me what I am!

DEAN (*with dawning dread*): —I—?

MRS. DEAN (*twisted smile*): Mm . . . Oh, you've been very good, dear, marvelously good, but goodness isn't the same animal; no, indeed it is not. . . . (*Kindly*) You can't bear the sight of me. . . . Did you think I didn't know?

DEAN (*appalled*): Not true! (*He grasps her wrist*)

MRS. DEAN (*She looks at it. Then as one recording an interesting phenomenon*): When you touch me, I can *feel* the goodness in your fingers. (*He lets go, she rises and goes to the table. In the same interested tone*) Why does he have to be so good, just to touch me? (*Now in a tone of thrill, almost pride*) And the answer—no. I didn't know the answer then, but I felt it (*she touches herself*) get to its feet. (*Tone of interest again*) Then later when you *talked to* me, I could hear the goodness in your voice and I wondered. (*Fearful again*) Why does he have to be good, just to talk to me?

16

DEAN: Not true!

MRS. DEAN (*thrill*): And it came towards me. (*The interest intensifies to horrified fascination*) Why does he never associate with me? Why have we never, never, never in anything been together? (*Pride*) And the answer (*Triumph*) Sprang! . . . (*Straightforward narrative*) Into the dreams, and when the dreams came into the day, I *was* the answer . . . (*Desolate*) "Gracious me," I thought, "a man who is the very lettering of sanity; married to me who have always been evil, and am now mad. No wonder he keeps what distance he can." (*Sits by table. Idly she picks up the shears*)

Omit all Dean's lines.

UNCLE VANYA

Anton Chekhov, *translated by Elisaveta Fen*

Yeliena, a young woman of beauty and intelligence, is the second wife of a retired professor. Sonia, her stepdaughter, has just admitted to her that she is in love with Astrov, a doctor. In this speech, Yeliena reveals her boredom with country life and discovers that she is half in love with Astrov herself.

ACT III

YELIENA (*alone*): There's nothing worse than knowing someone's secret and not being able to help. (*Musing*) He's not in love with her, that's obvious—but why shouldn't he marry her? She's not pretty, but she'd make an excellent wife for a country doctor at his time of life. She's intelligent, and so kind and pure. . . . No, that's not the point. . . . (*A pause*) I understand the poor girl so well. In the middle of all this desperate boredom, with just gray shadows wandering around

17

instead of human beings, with nothing but commonplace tittle-tattle to listen to from people who do nothing but eat, drink and sleep, he appears from time to time—so different from the rest of them, handsome, interesting, attractive, like a bright moon arising in the darkness. . . . To fall under the fascination of a man like that, to forget oneself. . . . I believe I'm a little attracted myself. . . . Yes, I'm bored when he's not about, and here I am smiling when I think of him. . . . Uncle Vanya here says I have mermaid's blood in my veins. "Let yourself go for once in your life." . . . Well, perhaps that's what I ought to do. . . . To fly away, free as a bird, away from all of you, from your sleepy faces and talk, to forget that you exist at all—every one of you! . . . But I'm too timid and shy. . . . My conscience would torment me to distraction. . . . He comes here every day. . . . I can guess why he comes and already I feel guilty. . . . I want to fall on my knees before Sonia, to ask her forgiveness and cry. . . .

THE LITTLE FOXES

Lillian Hellman

The scene is a small town in the deep South, the spring of 1900. Birdie is a gentle woman of about forty, well bred and somewhat faded. Oscar Hubbard married her as part of a business deal and now either ignores her or bullies her. She is too timid to oppose her circumstances; instead, she drinks. She has had several glasses of elderberry wine and is snatching at little bits of remembered happiness.

ACT III

BIRDIE: I remember. It was my first big party, at Lionnet I mean, and I was so excited, and there I was with hiccoughs and Mama laughing. (*Softly. Looking at carafe*) Mama always laughed. (*Picks up carafe*) A big party, a lovely dress from Mr. Worth in Paris, France, and hiccoughs. (*Pours drink*) My brother pounding me on the back and Mama with the elderberry bottle, laughing at me. Everybody was on their way to come, and I was such a ninny, hiccoughing away. (*Drinks*) You know, that was the first day I ever saw Oscar Hubbard. The Ballongs were selling their horses and he was going there to buy. He passed and lifted his hat—we could see him from the window—and my brother, to tease Mama, said maybe we should have invited the Hubbards to the party. He said Mama didn't like them because they kept a store, and he said that was old-fashioned of her. (*Her face lights up*) And then, and *then*, I saw Mama angry for the first time in my life. She said that wasn't the reason. She said she was old-fashioned, but not that way. She said she was old-fashioned enough not to like people who killed animals they couldn't use, and who made their money charging awful interest to poor, ignorant niggers and cheating them on what they bought. She was very angry, Mama was. I had never seen her face like that. And then suddenly she laughed and said, "Look, I've frightened Birdie out of the hiccoughs." (*Her head drops. Then softly*) And so she had. They were all gone. (*Moves to sofa, sits*)

BLUES FOR MISTER CHARLIE

James Baldwin

Blues is concerned with the murder of a young black man by a
white shopkeeper in a small Southern town and the effects of
the act upon a number of townspeople.

Richard, the son of the town's black minister, comes home
from New York to lick his wounds. He has recently been withdrawn from heroin addiction and is restless and unhappy.
Juanita, whom he knew as a child, is now working for a civil
rights project in the area. They are immediately drawn to one
another, but before their relationship reaches any level of
stability Richard is shot.

The contradictions in Richard's character, his loves and hates,
brash antagonism and personal insecurity, so reflect the town's
own illnesses that he becomes the catalyst for its explosion, the
victim of that explosion. Richard's advent and departure have
changed Juanita's life, and in this speech she tells Pete, a
friend, why she cannot love him.

For the actress, the fact that Juanita is black matters less than
the fact that she is a "nice" girl who has been overwhelmed by
sudden extremes of emotion and experience.

ACT I

JUANITA: When Richard came, he—*hit*—me in someplace
where I'd never been touched before. I don't mean—just
physically. He took all my attention—the deepest attention,
maybe, that one person can give another. He needed me
and he made a difference for me in this terrible world—do
you see what I mean? And—it's funny—when I was with
him, I didn't think of the future, I didn't dare. I didn't know
if I could be strong enough to give him what he needed for
as long as he would need it. It only lasted four or five days,
Pete—four or five days, like a storm, like lightning! And what
I saw during that storm I'll always see. Before that—I thought
I knew who I was. But now I know that there are more

things in me than I'll ever understand—and if I can't be faithful to myself, I'm afraid to promise I'll be faithful to one man!

ICARUS'S MOTHER
Sam Shepard

What happens in *Icarus* is quite clear: Five people are at a beach picnic. There are to be fireworks later in the evening. A plane is flying over the beach. The picnickers scream and wave at it. Later the two girls encounter the plane again on their walk up the beach. Finally the plane crashes into the sea and one of the characters has a long Greek-messenger speech about the crash and three rush off to see the wreck, while the other two remain, staring at the audience. The language is contemporary and natural, but the play is filled with rumblings of unmentioned terrors and cosmic preoccupations. It is extremely affecting to watch, although few of the audience would agree on just what the play is about.

Before this speech Pat has been somewhat victimized by the other members of the group. Her defense of the fireworks is also her defense of her own integrity and identity.

ONE-ACT PLAY
PAT: They get better and better as the years go by. It's true that some of them didn't work last year and that the city got gypped by the firecracker company. But that doesn't mean it will happen again this year. Besides, as Bill said, some of them were beautiful. It's worth it just to see one beautiful one out of all the duds. If none of them work except just one it will be worth it to see just that one beauti-

ful flashing thing across the whole sky. I'll wait all night on my back, even if they have to go through the whole stack without one of them working. Even if it's the very, very last one in the whole pile and everybody who came to see them left and went home. Even if I'm the only one left in the whole park and even if all the men who launch the firecrackers go home in despair and anguish and humiliation. I'll go down there myself and hook up the thing by myself and fire the thing without any help and run back up here and lie on my back and wait and listen and watch the god-damn thing explode all over the sky and watch it change colors and make all its sounds and do all the things that a firecracker's supposed to do. Then I'll watch it fizzle out and I'll get up slowly and brush the grass off my legs and walk back home and all the people will say what a lucky girl. What a lucky, lucky girl.

CHARACTER
AND DIALECT

ALL GOD'S CHILLUN GOT WINGS
Eugene O'Neill

Ella is a white girl married to Jim, a black man. Her accent is that of a poor district in New York. Jim has taken a law examination and is anxiously waiting for the result. Ella has become progressively more unbalanced since her marriage to him and at this point in the play has become subject to murderous fits of mania, punctuated with more lucid moments.

ACT II, SCENE iii
The scene is a flat of the better sort in the Negro district. The sun has just gone down. The spring twilight sheds a vague, gray light about the room, picking out the Congo mask on the stand by the window. The walls have shrunken in still more, the ceiling now barely clears the people's heads, the furniture and the characters appear enormously magnified. Law books are stacked in two great piles on each side of the table. Ella comes in from the right, the carving knife in her hand. She is pitifully thin, her face is wasted, but her eyes glow with a mad energy, her movements are abrupt and springlike. She looks stealthily about the room, then advances and stands before the mask, her arms akimbo, her attitude one of crazy mockery, fear and bravado. She is dressed in the

23

red dressing-gown, grown dirty and ragged now, and is in her bare feet.

ELLA: I'll give you the laugh, wait and see! (*Then in a confidential tone*) He thought I was asleep! He called, Ella, Ella—but I kept my eyes shut, I pretended to snore. I fooled him good. (*She gives a little hoarse laugh*) This is the first time he's dared to leave me alone for months and months. I've been wanting to talk to you every day, but this is the only chance—(*With sudden violence—flourishing her knife*) What're you grinning about, you dirty nigger, you? How dare you grin at me? I guess you forget what you are! That's always the way. Be kind to you, treat you decent, and in a second you've got a swelled head, you think you're somebody, you're all over the place putting on airs. Why, it's got so I can't even walk down the street without seeing niggers, niggers everywhere. Hanging around, grinning, grinning—going to school—pretending they're white—taking examinations— (*She stops, arrested by the word, then suddenly*) That's where he's gone—down to the mail-box—to see if there's a letter from the Board—telling him—but why is he so long? (*She calls pitifully*) Jim! (*Then in a terrified whimper*) Maybe he's passed! Maybe he's passed! (*In a frenzy*) No! No! He can't! I'd kill him! I'd kill him! I'd kill myself! (*Threatening the Congo mask*) It's you who're to blame for this! Yes, you! Oh, I'm on to you! (*Then appealingly*) But why d'you want to do this to us? What have I ever done wrong to you? What have you got against me? I married you, didn't I? Why don't you let Jim alone? Why don't you let him be happy as he is—with me? Why don't you let me be happy? He's white, isn't he—the whitest man that ever lived? Where do you come in to interfere? Black! Black! Black as dirt! You've poisoned me! I can't wash myself clean! Oh, I hate you! I hate you! Why don't you let Jim and I be happy? (*She sinks down in his chair, her arms outstretched on the table*)

ANDORRA

Max Frisch, *translated by Michael Bullock*

The characters in this play are types. The author says that "they should be played in such a way that the spectator at first likes, or at least tolerates, them, since they all appear innocuous and that he always sees them in their true light rather too late, as in real life."

The Señora, a woman from over the border, is visiting Andorra and has put up at the inn. In this scene she is speaking to her son, Andri. He does not know that she is his mother and believes himself to be a Jew and the foster child of the Teacher. After this speech the Señora kisses him good-by and leaves. She is stoned in the street and her dead body is brought onto the stage at the end of the scene.

SCENE 9

SENORA: I ought to go now. (*She remains seated*) When I was your age—that goes very quickly, Andri; you're twenty now and can't believe it: people meet, love, part, life is in front of you, and when you look in the mirror, suddenly it is behind you. You don't seem to yourself very different, but suddenly it is other people who are twenty. . . . When I was your age—my father, an officer, had been killed in the war. I knew how he thought, and I didn't want to think like him. We wanted a different world. We were young like you, and what we were taught was murderous, we knew that. And we despised the world as it is, we saw through it and dared to want another one. And we tried to create another one. We wanted not to be afraid of people. Not about anything in the world. We didn't want to lie. When we saw that we were merely keeping silent about our fear, we hated each other. Our new world didn't last long. We crossed the frontiers again, back to where we had come from when we were as young as you. . . . (*She rises*) Do you understand what I'm saying?

CHICKEN SOUP WITH BARLEY
Arnold Wesker

This play is the first in Arnold Wesker's trilogy about the Kahn family. Sarah is Jewish and of European origin. She is fifty-six and showing signs of her age; her life has not been an easy one. But something of her old fire remains. Sarah has had very little education and lacks imagination in some ways, but there is a kind of nobility about her, something matriarchal. Harry, her work-shy husband, has had two strokes and has now become incontinent and senile. Her tone when she talks about him in this scene is compassionate. Harry has dozed off in his chair and she is talking to two friends, Bessie and Monty Blatt. This act of the play is set in a public housing flat in Hackney.

ACT III, SCENE i

SARAH: It's not easy for him. But he won't do anything to help himself. I don't know, other men get ill but they fight. Harry's never fought. Funny thing. There were three men like this in the flats, all had strokes. And all three of them seemed to look the same. They walked the same, stooped the same and all needing a shave. They used to sit outside together and talk for hours on end and smoke. Sit and talk and smoke. That was their life. Then one day one of them decided he wanted to live so he gets up and finds himself a job—running a small shoe-mender's—and he's earning money now. A miracle! Just like that. But the other one—he wanted to die. I used to see him standing outside in the rain, the pouring rain, getting all wet so that he could catch a cold and die. Well, it happened; last week he died. Influenza! He just didn't want to live. But Harry was not like either of them. He didn't want to die but he doesn't seem to care about living. So! What can you do to help a man like that? I make his food and I buy him cigarettes and he's happy. My only dread is that he will mess himself. When that happens I go mad—I just don't know what I'm doing.

THE ENTERTAINER

John Osborne

Phoebe is the second wife of Archie Rice, a fifth-rate music hall comedian. They are living in seedy rooms. She is about sixty, still concerned about her appearance in that she takes trouble with her hair-styles and uses make-up, but not very well. She is a restless character who finds it difficult to concentrate. In this scene she is excited at her stepdaughter Jean's unexpected arrival. She is talking to Jean and to Archie's father, Billy, who lives with them.

NO. 3

PHOEBE (*laughs*): Blimey, you should know better than to ask me that! You know what a rotten memory I've got. Well, cheerio! (*She drinks*) OOOh, that's a nice drop of gin—some of the muck they give you nowadays—taste like cheap scent some of it. You should hear him going on about the beer. No, they've got a lot of rubbish on at the pictures these days. I haven't seen a decent picture for ages. It seems to be all bands or singing. Either that or Westerns. He doesn't mind them so much. But I can't stand all that shooting. It gives me a headache. But I'm dreadful; if there's nothing else on, I still go just the same, don't I? Even if it is just to the bug house round the corner. I get myself six pennorth of sweets and have a couple of hours, whatever's on. I hear they're closing that place down, by the way. Everything's doing badly. That's what I tell Archie. Course he gets worried because the business is bad. Still that's how it is, people haven't got the money, have they? I'm at Woolworth's now, did I tell you? I'm on the electrical counter. It's not bad. Girls are a bit common, that's all. Oh, it is nice to see you. Archie will be so pleased. She looks a bit peaky. Round the face, don't you think? Don't you think she looks a bit peaky?

JUNO AND THE PAYCOCK

Sean O'Casey

The play is set in 1922 in the slums of Dublin. Mrs. Madigan, a woman of about forty-five, is a friend of Juno. She has called in to see her. Sean O'Casey has given this description of the character. "When others say anything or following a statement made by herself, she has a habit of putting her head a little to one side and nodding it rapidly several times in succession like a bird pecking at a hard berry. Indeed she has a good deal of the bird in her, but the bird instinct is by no means a melodious one. She is ignorant, vulgar and forward but her heart is generous withal." Juno, Mary Boyle, Joxer and Bentham are present in this scene.

ACT II

MRS. MADIGAN: Gawn with you, child, an' you only goin' to be marrid; I remember as well as I remember yestherday—it was on a lovely August evenin', exactly accordin' to date, fifteen years ago come the Tuesday folleyin' the nex' that's comin' on, when me own man (the Lord be good to him) an' me was sittin' shy together in a doty little nook on a counthry road, adjacent to The Stiles. "That'll scratch your lovely, little white neck" says he, ketchin' hould of a danglin' bramble branch, holdin' clusters of the loveliest flowers you ever seen, an' breakin' it off, so that his arm fell, accidental like, roun' me waist, an' as I felt it tightenin', an' tightenin', an' tightenin', I thought me buzzum was every minute goin' to burst out into a roystherin' song about

The little green leaves that were shakin' on the threes,

The gallivantin' buttherflies, an' buzzin' o' the bees!

BOYLE: Ordher for the song!

JUNO: Come on, Mary—we'll do our best.

(*Juno and Mary stand up, and choosing a suitable position, sing simply "Home to Our Mountains." They bow to the company, and return to their places*)

BOYLE (*emotionally, at the end of song*): Lull . . . me . . . to . . . rest!

JOXER (*clapping his hands*): Bravo! bravo! Darlin' girulls, darlin' girulls!

MRS. MADIGAN: Juno, I never seen you in betther form.

BENTHAM: Very nicely rendered indeed.

MRS. MADIGAN: A noble call, a noble call!

MRS. BOYLE: What about yourself, Mrs. Madigan?

(*After some coaxing, MRS. MADIGAN rises and in a quivering voice sings the following verse*):

If I were a blackbird I'd whistle and sing;

I'd follow the ship that my thrue love was in;

An' on the top riggin', I'd there build me nest,

An' at night I would sleep on my Willie's white breast!

(*Becoming husky, amid applause, she sits down*)

MRS. MADIGAN: Ah, me voice is too husky now, Juno; though I remember the time when Maisie Madigan could sing like a nightingale at matin' time. I remember as well as I remember yestherday, at a party given to celebrate the comin' of the first chiselur to Annie an' Benny Jimeson—who was the barber, yous may remember, in Henrietta Street, that, afther Easter Week, hung out a green, white an' orange pole, an' then, when the Tans started their Jazz dancin,' whipped it in agen, an' stuck out a red, white an' blue wan instead, givin' as an excuse that a barber's pole was strictly non-political—singin' "An You'll Remember Me," with the top notes quiverin' in a dead hush of pethrified attention, folleyed by a clappin' o' han's that shuk the tumblers on the table, an' capped be Jimeson, the barber, say'n that it was the best rendherin' of "You'll Remember Me" he ever heard in his natural!

Omit from end of Mrs. Madigan's line "an buzzin' o' the bees!" to end of Mrs. Boyle's line "What about yourself, Mrs. Madigan?"

KING HENRY V

William Shakespeare

The scene is Eastcheap, before the Boar's Head tavern. The hostess of the Boar's Head, formerly Mistress Quickly, is now married to Pistol. Here she is describing Falstaff's death to some of his boon companions, Pistol, Nym and Bardolph, before they leave to join King Henry V's army which is bound for France.

ACT II, SCENE iii

HOSTESS: Nay, sure, he's not in hell: he's in Arthur's bosom, if ever man went to Arthur's bosom. 'A made a finer end, and went away, an it had been any christom child; 'a parted ev'n just between twelve and one, ev'n at the turning o' th' tide: for after I saw him fumble with the sheets, and play with flowers, and smile upon his fingers' ends, I knew there was but one way; for his nose was as sharp as a pen, and 'a babbled of green fields. "How now, Sir John!" quoth I: "what, man! be o' good cheer." So 'a cried out "God, God, God!" three or four times. Now I, to comfort him, bid him 'a should not think of God; I hoped there was no need to trouble himself with any such thoughts yet. So 'a bade me lay more clothes on his feet: I put my hands into the bed and felt them, and they were as cold as any stone; then I felt to his knees, and so upward and upward, and all was as cold as any stone.

POINT OF DEPARTURE

Jean Anouilh, *translated by Kitty Black*

Mother is a professional actress who has spent her life on second-rate tours. Anouilh says of her, "Ever since 1920 she has grown younger every day." The play is inspired by the legend of Orpheus and Eurydice. The first act is set in a provincial French railway station where the theatrical company is waiting for a connection. Mother addresses her remarks to her daughter Eurydice and to the waiter.

ACT I

MOTHER *enters UL. Ever since 1920 she has grown younger every day. She sees EURYDICE through the windows and comes in through the swing doors, fanning herself with a handkerchief. She moves to the table LC and sits in the chair R of it.*

MOTHER: This heat. How I hate waiting at stations. The whole tour has been a disgrace—as usual. The manager ought to arrange that the leading actors don't spend all their time waiting for connections. When you've spent the whole day on a platform how can you give your best in the evening.

EURYDICE (*replacing her comb and mirror in her bag*): There's only one train for the whole company and it's an hour late because of the storm yesterday. The manager can't help it.

MOTHER: You always find excuses for these incompetents. (*The WAITER enters by the service door and moves to the table LC*)

WAITER: May I take your order, ladies?

MOTHER: Do you feel like something?

EURYDICE: After that star entrance of yours, it's the least we can do.

MOTHER (*to the WAITER*): Have you any really good peppermint?

WAITER: Yes, madame.

MOTHER: I'll have a peppermint. In Argentine, or in Brazil, when the heat was really exhausting I always used to take a peppermint just before making my first entrance. Sarah gave me the tip. A peppermint. (*ORPHEUS rises, picks up his accordion, goes to the desk, pays the bill, then goes out through the swing doors and exits L.*)

WAITER: And for mademoiselle?

EURYDICE: Coffee, please.

(*The WAITER exits by the service door. The group on the platform breaks up. The two girls exit to R, MOLAC and the MANAGER exit to L*)

MOTHER: Why aren't you with Mathias? He's wandering about like a soul in torment.

EURYDICE: Don't worry about him.

MOTHER: It was very wrong of you to upset that boy. He adores you. It was your fault in the first place. You shouldn't have let him be your lover. I told you so at the time, but it's too late to worry about that now. Besides, we all begin and end with actors. When I was your age, I was much prettier than you. I could have been had by anyone I pleased. All I could do was waste my time with your father. You see the charming results yourself.

(*The WAITER enters by the service door. He carries a tray with a glass of peppermint and cup of coffee. He moves to the table LC and puts the drinks on it*)

WAITER: A little ice, madame?

MOTHER: Never—think of my voice.

(*The WAITER exits by the service door*)

(*She tastes the peppermint*) This peppermint is disgusting. I hate the provinces, I hate these second-rate towns. But in Paris nowadays, they only go mad over little idiots with no breasts, who can't say three words without fluffing. What has the boy done to upset you? You didn't even get into the same compartment at Montélimar. My dear child, a

32

mother is a girl's natural confidante, particularly when they're the same age—(*EURYDICE gives MOTHER a withering look*) I mean, particularly when she's a very young mother. Come along, dear, tell me. What has he done?

Omit Eurydice's and waiter's lines.

A RAISIN IN THE SUN
Lorraine Hansberry

The play is set in Chicago's Southside sometime between World War II and the present. The action takes place in a shabby living room. Mama is a strong, robust woman in her early sixties. She has a strong face and a nobility of bearing. Her speech is careless and somewhat slurred and her voice soft. In this scene she is talking to her daughter-in-law, Ruth.

ACT 1, SCENE i

MAMA (*looking up at the words "rat trap" and then looking around and sighing—in a suddenly reflective mood*): "Rat trap"—yes, that's all it is. (*Smiling*) I remember just as well the day me and Big Walter moved in here. Hadn't been married but two weeks and wasn't planning on living here no more than a year. (*She shakes her head at the dissolved dream*) We was going to set away, little by little, don't you know, and buy a little place out in Morgan Park. We had even picked out the house. (*Chuckling a little*) Looks right dumpy today. But Lord, child, you should know all the dreams I had 'bout buying that house and fixing it up and making me a little garden in the back—(*She waits and stops smiling*) And didn't none of it happen. (*She drops her hands in a futile gesture*)

33

RUTH (*keeps her head down, ironing*): Yes, life can be a barrel of disappointments, sometimes.

MAMA: Honey, Big Walter would come in here some nights back then and slump down on that couch there and just look at the rug, and look at me and look at the rug and then back at me—and I'd know he was down then . . . really down. (*After a second very long and thoughtful pause; she is seeing back to times that only she can see*) And then, Lord, when I lost that baby—little Claude—I almost thought I was going to lose Big Walter too. Oh, that man grieved hisself! He was one man to love his children.

RUTH: Ain't nothin' can tear at you like losin' your baby.

MAMA: I guess that's how come that man finally worked hisself to death like he done. Like he was fighting his own war with this here world that took his baby from him.

RUTH: He sure was a fine man, all right. I always liked Mr. Younger.

MAMA: Crazy 'bout his children! God knows there was plenty wrong with Walter Younger—hard-headed, mean, kind of wild with women—plenty wrong with him. But he sure loved his children. Always wanted them to have something—be something. That's where Brother gets all these notions, I reckon. Big Walter used to say, he'd get right wet in the eyes sometimes, lean his head back with the water standing in his eyes and say, "Seems like God didn't see fit to give the black man nothing but dreams—but He did give us children to make them dreams seem worthwhile." (*She smiles*) He could talk like that, don't you know.

Omit Ruth's lines.

ROBERT'S WIFE

St. John Ervine

Mrs. Jones is a working-class mother. The bishop and the vicar have persuaded her to give her consent to her boy Dick's marriage to a worthless girl who is going to have his baby. Reluctantly Mrs. Jones has agreed to the marriage. Now she returns to the vicarage to tell them that the baby has died. In this scene she is speaking to the bishop and to the vicar and his wife.

ACT II, SCENE ii

ROBERT: Is there anything we can do, Mrs. Jones?

MRS. JONES: No, sir, nothin'. I dunno why I come, really . . . 'cept I just thought I would. Seems so funny, some'ow, us all makin' that fuss about gettin' Dick an' 'Ilda married, an' now the baby's dead, an' my boy's tied to that girl for life. Silly, ain't it? (*To the* BISHOP) You know, sir, she's no good. She's a foolish girl. She didn't ought to be allowed to marry any man. Just a fool, sir. I looked at 'er this mornin' after 'er baby was dead, an' I thought to myself, "Huh, my girl, two trips to the pictures an' you'll forget all about this!" I s'pose I oughtn't to blame 'er, really. She can't 'elp bein' a fool. Nobody wants to be one. But I do wish she'd married some other chap than my boy. It was a mistake, sir. We didn't ought to mess about with other people's lives. We didn't ought. Why can't we leave each other alone? (*She begins to cry, and, in her distress, turns and stumbles from the room*)

Omit Robert's line.

ROOTS

Arnold Wesker

Roots is the second play in Wesker's famous trilogy. It follows *Chicken Soup with Barley*. In this scene, set in a ramshackle house in Norfolk, Beatie, the twenty-two-year-old daughter of a Norfolk farmhand, is visiting her sister, Jenny, and her brother-in-law. She has been working in London where she has met an intellectual called Ronnie. She has come back to Norfolk for a holiday.

ACT I

BEATIE (*loudly*): It's not true! We're in love! (*Softly*) No, I don't know. I won't know till he come here. From the first day I went to work as waitress in the Dell Hotel and saw him working in the kitchen I fell in love—and I thought it was easy. I thought everything was easy. I chased him for three months with compliments and presents until I finally give myself to him. He never said he love me nor I didn't care but once he had taken me he seemed to think he was responsible for me and I told him no different. I'd make him love me I thought. I didn't know much about him except he was different and used to write most of the time. And then he went back to London and I followed him there. (*Rising and crossing slowly DL*) I've never moved far from home but I did for him and he felt all the time he couldn't leave me and I didn't tell him no different. And then I got to know more about him. He was interested in all the things I never ever thought about. About politics and art and all that, and he tried to teach me. He's a socialist and he used to say you couldn't bring socialism to a country by making speeches, but perhaps you could pass it on to someone who was near to you. So I pretended I was

36

interested—but I didn't understand much. All the time he's trying to teach me but I can't take it, Jenny. And yet, at the same time, I want to show I'm willing. I'm not used to learning. Learning was at school and that's finished with.

THE SHADOW OF THE GLEN

J. M. Synge

The scene is the last cottage at the head of a long glen in County Wicklow. Nora's husband, supposedly dead, is lying on a bed in the corner covered with a sheet. A tramp arrives at the door and she asks him in out of the rain. Later, Nora goes out to find a young herdsman, Michael Dara, and brings him back. During the scene she is giving Michael tea and they are counting the husband's money.

NORA (*giving him his tea*): It's in a lonesome place you do have to be talking with someone, and looking for someone, in the evening of the day, and if it's a power of men I'm after knowing they were fine men, for I was a hard child to please, and a hard girl to please (*she looks at him a little sternly*), and it's a hard woman I am to please this day, Michael Dara, and it's no lie I'm telling you.

MICHAEL (*looking over to see that the tramp is asleep, and then pointing to the dead man*): Was it a hard woman to please you were when you took himself for your man?

NORA (*taking the stocking with the money from her pocket, and putting it on the table*): I do be thinking in the long nights it was a big fool I was that time, Michael Dara; for what good is a bit of a farm with cows on it, and sheep on

37

the back hills, when you do be sitting looking out from a door, and seeing nothing but the mists rolling down the bog, and the mists again and they rolling up the bog, and hear nothing but the wind crying out in the bits of broken trees were left from a great storm, and the streams roaring with the rain.

MICHAEL (*looking at her uneasily*): What is it ails you this night, Nora Burke? I've heard tell it's the like of that talk you do hear from men, and they after being a great while on the back hills.

NORA (*putting the money on the table*): It's a bad night and a wild night, Michael Dara, and isn't it a great while I am at the foot of the back hills, sitting up here boiling food for himself, and food for the brood sow, and baking a cake when the night falls? (*She puts up the money listlessly in little piles on the table*) Isn't it a long while I am sitting here in the winter and the summer, and the fine spring, with the young growing behind me and the old passing, saying to myself one time to look on Mary Brien, who wasn't that height (*holding out her hand*), and I a fine girl growing up, and there she is now with two children, and another coming on her in three months or four. (*She pauses*)

MICHAEL (*moving over three of the piles*): That's three pounds we have now, Nora Burke.

NORA (*continuing in the same voice*): And saying to myself another time, to look on Peggy Cavanagh, who had the lightest hand at milking a cow that wouldn't be easy, or turning a cake, and there she is now walking round on the roads, or sitting in a dirty old house, with no teeth in her mouth, and no sense, and no more hair than you'd see on a bit of a hill and they after burning the furze from it.

MICHAEL: That's five pounds and ten notes, a good sum surely! . . . It's not that way you'll be talking when you marry a young man, Nora Burke, and they were saying in the fair my lambs were the best lambs, and I got a grand price, for I'm no fool now at making a bargain when my lambs are good.

NORA: What was it you got?

MICHAEL: Twenty pounds for the lot, Nora Burke. . . . We'd do right to wait now till himself will be quiet awhile in the Seven Churches, and then you'll marry me in the chapel of Rathvanna, and I'll bring the sheep up on the bit of a hill you have on the back mountain, and we won't have anything we'd be afeared to let our minds on when the mist is down.

NORA (*pouring him out some whisky*): Why would I marry you, Mike Dara? You'll be getting old and I'll be getting old, and in a little while, I'm telling you, you'll be sitting up in your bed—the way himself was sitting—with a shake in your face, and your teeth falling, and the white hair sticking out round you like an old bush where sheep do be leaping a gap. (*Dan Burke sits up noiselessly from under the sheet, with his hand to his face. His white hair is sticking out round his head. Nora goes on slowly without hearing him*) It's a pitiful thing to be getting old, but it's a queer thing surely. It's a queer thing to see an old man sitting up there in his bed with no teeth in him, and a rough word in his mouth, and his chin the way it would take the bark from the edge of an oak board you'd have building a door. . . . God forgive me, Michael Dara, we'll all be getting old, but it's a queer thing surely.

Omit all Michael's lines and Nora's "What was it you got?"

SOMETHING UNSPOKEN

Tennessee Williams

The play is set in the Garden District of New Orleans. Here Cornelia Scott lives with her companion, Grace Lancaster. Cornelia, a formidable woman of sixty, is speaking on the telephone to Esmeralda, one of the Daughters of the club in which Cornelia has held office. She is desperately anxious to be re-elected and the speech reveals considerable tension.

CORNELIA (*into phone*): Are you upstairs now, dear? Well, I wondered. It took you so long to call back. Oh, but I thought you said the luncheon was over. Well, I'm glad that you fortified yourself with a bite to eat. What did the buffet consist of? Chicken à la king! Wouldn't you know it! That is so characteristic of poor Amelia! With bits of pimento and tiny mushrooms in it? What did the ladies counting their calories do! Nibbled around the edges? Oh, poor dears!—and afterwards I suppose there was lemon sherbert with ladyfingers? What, lime sherbert! And *no* ladyfingers? *What a departure!* What a *shocking* apostasy! I'm quite stunned! Ho ho ho . . . (*Reaches shakily for cup*) —Now what's going on? Discussing the Civil Rights Program? Then they won't take the vote for at least half an hour!—Now, Esmeralda, I *do* hope you understand my position clearly. I don't wish to hold any office in the Chapter unless it's by acclamation. You know what that means, don't you? It's a parliamentary term. It means when someone is desired for an office so unanimously that no vote has to be taken. In other words, elected automatically, simply by nomination, unopposed. Yes, my dear; it's just as simple as that. I have served as Treasurer for three terms, twice as Secretary, once as Chaplain—and what a dreary office that was with those long-drawn prayers for the Confederate dead! Altogether I've served on the Board for, let's see, fourteen years!—Well, now, my dear, the point is simply this. If the Daughters feel that I have demonstrated my capabilities and loyalty strongly enough that I should simply be named as Regent without a vote being taken—by unanimous acclamation!—why, then, of course I would feel obliged to accept. . . . (*Her voice trembles with emotion*) But if, on the other hand, the—uh—*clique!*—and you know the ones I mean!—is bold enough to propose someone else for the office—Do you understand my position? In that eventuality, hard as it is to imagine—I prefer to bow out of the picture entirely!—The moment another nomination is made and seconded, my own must be withdrawn, at once, unconditionally! Is that quite understood, Esmeralda? Then good! Go back downstairs to the meeting. Digest your chicken à la king, my dear, and call me again on the upstairs phone as soon as there's something to tell me.

UNDER MILK WOOD

Dylan Thomas

These two characters from *Under Milk Wood* give opportunity for vocal contrast; Mrs. Dai Bread One, relaxed and comfortable, Mrs. Dai Bread Two, provocative in a gypsy way. Both live in the small Welsh town by the sea that Dylan Thomas described in this play that was originally written for radio performance. The play covers a day in the life of the small community and these speeches come from the early part where the town is waking up.

MRS. DAI BREAD ONE: Me, Mrs. Dai Bread One, capped and shawled and no old corset, nice to be comfy, nice to be nice clogging on the cobbles to stir up a neighbor. Oh, Mrs. Sarah, can you spare a loaf, love? Dai Bread forgot the bread. There's a lovely morning! How's your boils this morning? Isn't that good news now, it's a change to sit down. Ta, Mrs. Sarah.

MRS. DAI BREAD TWO: Me, Mrs. Dai Bread Two, gypsied to kill in a silky scarlet petticoat above my knees, dirty pretty knees, see my body through my petticoat brown as a berry, high-heel shoes with one heel missing, tortoise-shell comb in my bright black slinky hair, nothing else at all but a dab of scent, lolling gaudy at the doorway, tell your fortune in the tea leaves scowling at the sunshine, lighting up my pipe.

TITUBA'S CHILDREN

William Carlos Williams

The play takes place in Salem, Massachusetts, 1692, and Washington, D.C., 1950, both scenes of witch hunts. The Salem scenes are based on source material, which Williams has infused with dramatic vitality.

Tituba, "a drawling half-Negro, half-Carib slave," has been enlisted by a group of hysterical adolescent girls in their malicious play at witchcraft.

The girls are coaxing her to tell about the magic of her country, while she croons to a young child whom she is later accused of having bewitched. The girl is sick, and Tituba longs to take her "away from this cold weather and these hard people." The speech is filled with her longing for her own home, and she loses herself in the rich imagery and flow of language.

ACT I, SCENE i

TITUBA: On the green islands they no snow—and no hard ice looks like a goat's horn. Like a stone. And the blue waves come soothin' in free and easy from the big bay and they smell sweet as bees' honey through the mango trees. (*The girls listen*) The night so deep and dark and full of big stars you get lost in it, and a big crawlin' flower hangs from the walls long as my arm, called the night bloomin' serious. A big, full flower and when it crack it shall creep down the wall like it have feet. And the richest smell like nothin' you ever smell on the earth roll out of it—and the big night come flyin' to it on wings a foot long, blue and green, come flyin' in to dip down and drink up the sky so sweet you don't dare lie down on the wall or they pull you up off you back and carry you to the hills—and you don't care what they do to you.

THE AMERICAN DREAM

Edward Albee

Albee calls this one-act play "an examination of the American scene," and adds that he hopes one finds the play offensive, as it was his intention to offend. For the strength of the play to be maintained the actor must be careful to play the characters, not the message. Mommy does not find herself a caricature, and it is to be hoped that the gentleman in the third row will recognize a little of himself in Daddy.

The play opens with Mommy and Daddy sitting on opposite sides of their exceedingly unpleasant living room. They are waiting to get satisfaction. Many years before, they purchased a child who proved unsatisfactory in many ways and finally

43

died. Now they want their money back. While waiting Mommy tells the following story.

Although the scene is broadly drawn the relationship between the characters is complex and should receive more than a cursory examination.

MOMMY (*giggles at the thought; then*): All right, now. I went to buy a new hat yesterday and I said, "I'd like a new hat, please." And so, they showed me a few hats, green ones and blue ones, and I didn't like any of them, not one bit. What did I say? What did I just say?

DADDY: You didn't like any of them, not one bit.

MOMMY: That's right; you just keep paying attention. And then they showed me one that I did like. It was a lovely little hat, and I said, "Oh, this is a lovely little hat; I'll take this hat; or my, it's lovely. What color is it?" And they said, "Why, this is beige; isn't it a lovely little beige hat?" And I said, "Oh, it's just lovely." And so, I bought it. (*Stops, looks at* DADDY)

DADDY (*to show he is paying attention*): And so you bought it.

MOMMY: And so I bought it, and I walked out of the store with the hat right on my head, and I ran spang into the chairman of our woman's club, and she said, "Oh, my dear, isn't that a lovely little hat? Where did you get that lovely little hat? It's the loveliest little hat; I've always wanted a wheat-colored hat *myself*." And, I said, "Why, no, my dear; this hat is beige; beige." And she laughed and said, "Why no, my dear, that's a wheat-colored hat . . . wheat. I know beige from wheat." And I said, "Well, my dear, I know beige from wheat, too." What did I say? What did I just say?

DADDY (*tonelessly*): Well, my dear, I know beige from wheat, too.

MOMMY: That's right. And she laughed, and she said, "Well, my dear, they certainly put one over on you. That's wheat if I ever saw wheat. But it's lovely, just the same." And then she walked off. She's a dreadful woman, you don't know her; she has dreadful taste, two dreadful children, a dreadful house, and an absolutely adorable husband who sits in a wheel chair all the time. You don't know him. You don't know anybody, do you? She's just a dreadful woman, but she *is* chairman of our woman's club, so naturally I'm terribly fond of her. So, I went right back into the hat shop, and I said, "Look here; what do you mean selling me a hat that you say is beige, when it's wheat all the time . . . wheat! I can tell beige from wheat any day in the week, but not in this artificial light of yours." They have artificial light, Daddy.

DADDY: Have they!

MOMMY: And I said, "The minute I got outside I could tell that it wasn't a beige hat at all; it was a wheat hat." And they said to me, "How could you tell that when you had the hat on the top of your head?" Well, that made me angry, and so I made a scene right there; I screamed as hard as I could; I took my hat off and I threw it down on the counter, and oh, I made a terrible scene. I said, I made a terrible scene.

DADDY (*snapping to*): Yes . . . yes . . . good for you!

MOMMY: And I made an absolutely terrible scene; and they became frightened, and they said, "Oh, madam; oh, madam." But I kept right on, and finally they admitted that they might have made a mistake; so they took my hat into the back, and then they came out again with a hat that looked exactly like it. I took one look at it, and I said, "This hat is wheat-colored; wheat." Well, of course, they said, "Oh, no, madam, this hat is beige; you go outside and see." So, I went outside, and lo and behold, it *was* beige. So I bought it.

DADDY (*clearing his throat*): I would imagine that it was the same hat they tried to sell you before.

45

MOMMY (*with a little laugh*): Well, of course it was!
DADDY: That's the way things are today; you just can't get satisfaction; you just try.
MOMMY: Well, *I* got satisfaction.

Omit Daddy's lines.

COMEDY

THE BEAUX' STRATAGEM

George Farquhar

The play is set near Lichfield at the beginning of the eighteenth century. Mrs. Sullen, wife to Squire Sullen, is London-bred and does not take kindly to country life. In this scene, in Lady Bountiful's house, she is talking to Dorinda, her husband's half-sister, and describing Sullen's drunkenness of the evening before.

ACT II, SCENE i

MRS. SULLEN: Country pleasures! Racks and torments! Dost think, child, that my limbs were made for leaping of ditches, and clambering over stiles? Or that my parents, wisely foreseeing my future happiness in country pleasures, had early instructed me in the rural accomplishments of drinking fat ale, playing at whisk, and smoking tobacco with my husband? or of spreading of plasters, brewing of diet-drinks, and stilling rosemary-water, with the good old gentle-woman my mother-in-law?

Not that I disapprove rural pleasures, as the poets have painted them; in their landscape, every Phillis has her Cory-don, every murmuring stream and every flowery mead give fresh alarms to love. Besides, you'll find that their couples were never married.—But yonder I see my Corydon, and a

47

sweet swain it is, Heaven knows! Come, Dorinda, don't be angry; he's my husband, and your brother; and between both, is he not a sad brute?

DORINDA: I have nothing to say to your part of him— you're the best judge.

MRS. SULLEN: O sister, sister! If ever you marry, beware of a sullen, silent sot, one that's always musing, but never thinks. There's some diversion in a talking blockhead; and since a woman must wear chains, I would have the pleasure of hearing 'em rattle a little. Now you shall see—but take this by the way: he came home this morning at his usual hour of four, wakened me out of a sweet dream of something else by tumbling over the tea-table, which he broke all to pieces; after his man and he had rolled about the room, like sick passengers in a storm, he comes flounce into bed, dead as a salmon into a fishmonger's basket; his feet cold as ice, his breath hot as a furnace, and his hands and his face as greasy as his flannel nightcap. O matrimony! He tosses up the clothes with a barbarous swing over his shoulders, disorders the whole economy of my bed, leaves me half naked, and my whole night's comfort is the tunable serenade of that wakeful nightingale, his nose! Oh, the pleasure of counting the melancholy clock by a snoring husband! But now, sister, you shall see how handsomely, being a well-bred man, he will beg my pardon.

Omit Dorinda's lines.

THE COMPLAISANT LOVER
Graham Greene

Mary, now in her middle thirties, has been married to Victor for sixteen years. She has become frustrated by the routine of domesticity. In this speech, she is talking to Clive Root, younger and more attractive than her husband and with whom she has fallen in love. She is planning to spend an illicit few days with him in Amsterdam, having told Victor that she is going with an imaginary friend called Jane Crane.

Mary enters. She goes to a telephone and dials a number. After a while a voice answers.

MARY: Clive. Are you alone? . . . I'm coming away with you, Clive . . . I only mean a holiday. Could you leave on the thirteenth? . . . No, we can't go there, it's too far for a short holiday, Clive—it's got to be Amsterdam . . . I can't tell you why now. It just has to be, Clive. It's the Venice of the north. . . . All right. If you don't want four days alone with me in Amsterdam, just say so. We can call it off. . . . If it does rain, Clive, what does it matter? We'll just stay in bed, drinking Bols, whatever that is. . . . Oh, he's quite happy about it. He thinks I'm going with someone called Jane Crane. . . . No, she doesn't exist . . . the name just came into my head. . . . What do you mean, "Jane, Jane, tall as a crane?" Why do you all have to make up verses about her? . . . I don't care if Edith Sitwell wrote them. I can't alter Jane's name now. . . . Clive, will you do the bookings? I'll pay you back, next month when my allowance comes in. Any hotel but the Amstel . . . I know it's the best, but someone I know is arriving there on the eighteenth. I don't want them mixed up. . . . You are happy, darling? . . . Yes, I am. . . . No we won't buy diamonds. . . . Did you say herrings? Raw herrings? . . . Oh, but I think raw herrings

sound fascinating and anything may happen, Clive, anything.
Even in Amsterdam.

The curtain falls as she talks.

THE COUNTRY WIFE
William Wycherley

Pinchwife has recently married Margery, a girl from the country.
He is extremely jealous and afraid that she will be tempted by
the licentious life in the London of Restoration times. Mr.
Horner, a notorious philanderer, has seen Margery at the play
and has told Pinchwife that he is attracted by her. Pinchwife
will only allow Margery to come to the New Exchange with him
if she dresses as a boy. Horner sees her there and suspects the
truth. He manages to see Margery on her own and presses passionate kisses on her. Later, Margery innocently tells her husband what has happened and he dictates a letter for her to
send to Horner scorning his advances and admitting that she
was in man's clothes.

When Pinchwife goes to find a candle and wax to seal the
letter, Margery writes the letter she is determined to send to
Horner instead of the one dictated to her by her husband.

MRS. PINCHWIFE: "For Mr. Horner"—So, I am glad he
has told me his name. Dear Mr. Horner! but why should I
send thee such a letter that will vex thee, and make thee
angry with me?—Well, I will not send it.—Ay, but then my
husband will kill me—for I see plainly he won't let me love
Mr. Horner—but what care I for my husband—but oh, what
if I writ at bottom my husband made me write it? Ay, but
then my husband would see't—Can one have no shift? ah,
a London woman would have had a hundred presently.

Stay—what if I should write a letter, and wrap it up like this, and write upon't too? Ay, but then my husband would see't. I don't know what to do.—But yet evads I'll try, so I will—for I will not send this letter to poor Mr. Horner, come what will on't. "Dear, sweet Mr. Horner"—(*Writes and repeats what she writes*)—so—"my husband would have me send you a base, rude unmannerly letter; but I won't"—so—"and would have me forbid you loving me; but I won't"—so—"and would have me say to you, I hate you, poor Mr. Horner; but I won't tell a lie for him"—there—"for I am sure if you and I were in the country at cards together"—so—"I could not help treading on your toe under the table"—so—"or rubbing knees with you, and staring in your face, till you saw me"—very well— "and then looking down, and blushing for an hour together"—so—"but I must make haste before my husband comes: and now he has taught me to write letters, you shall have longer ones from me, who am, dear, dear, poor, dear Mr. Horner, your most humble friend, and servant to command till death,—Margery Pinchwife."

Stay, I must give him a hint at bottom—so—now wrap it up just like t'other—so—now write "For Mr. Horner"—but oh now, what shall I do with it? for here comes my husband.

GILT AND GINGERBREAD
Lionel Hale

The time is the present; the setting a beautiful house in Regent's Park Terrace belonging to Mr. and Mrs. Yeyder. Louise Yeyder is a charming and elegant, if somewhat feather-headed woman of thirty-nine. This scene opens the play. She is sparkling with anger and full of determination as she speaks these lines to Mortimer Wilmot, a rival stockbroker of her husband's. Wilmot has pursued her back to the house.

ACT I

LOUISE (*beginning quietly*): I call it a damned outrage. (*She takes off a glove*) I am lunching perfectly quietly at the Ritz with a woman friend, and every time I try to look out at St. James's Park, there you are sitting at a table in the window by yourself, staring at me. You. A perfect stranger, staring. And you are still staring. I go off alone to the Curzon Cinema to see a film about two dwarfs making love in a cellar, in French; (*second glove off*) and I get bored with it, naturally enough, after half an hour, and I come out; and who seems to have got bored with it at the same moment and comes out too? You do. You. (*She takes off her hat*) I get into my car and am driven to South Molton Street to buy a hat. That hat. It's probably a perfectly dreadful hat, because I'm still upset about you and those two French dwarfs in a cellar. And I step into my car, and there you are halfway down South Molton Street, getting yourself a taxi. (*Leaves hat on arm of sofa. Crosses DL to mirror*) And when I arrive home, and let myself into my own front door— who calmly follows me in across my own hall and up my own stairs and into my own drawing room? (*Crosses back to sofa*) And there you stand! I have never been so insulted in my life. I don't know you from Adam; but your behavior is absolutely intolerable. It's unspeakable. It's entirely and utterly blackguardly.

Well, don't go! (*Vexed at herself, LOUISE sits down. She recaptures some of her affronted dignity*) I mean to say only that it seems the very worst of manners to go away without apologizing. I mean to say: it seems pretty cool to me— nobody asked you to sit down—Well, haven't you anything to say?

52

I AM A CAMERA

John Van Druten

The action of the play takes place in Fräulein Schneider's flat in Berlin in 1930, before the rise of the Hitler régime. Sally Bowles, young, gay and volatile, is talking to Christopher, a writer. Her mother has come to Berlin to bring Sally home, but has returned to England without her. Sally has promised to follow later. Despite her drifting promiscuous life in Berlin, Sally has retained a curious childlike innocence. She gives the impression of being a little girl trying to be wicked.

ACT III, SCENE iii

SALLY (*giggling a little*): Well, there is a man. He's wonderful, Chris. He really is. Two days ago. Just after we left here. He saw us in the street. . . . Mummy and me, I mean— and our eyes met—his and mine, I mean—and he sort of followed us. To a tea shop, where he sat and gazed at me. And back to the hotel. And at the restaurant. He had the table next to us, and he kept sort of hitching his foot around my chair. And he passed me a note in the fruit basket. Only Mummy got it by mistake. But it was in German; I told her it was from a film producer. And I went over and talked to him, and he *was*! Then we met later. He's quite marvelous, Chris. (*Kneels on couch*) He's got a long, black beard. Well, not really long. I've never been kissed by a beard before; I thought it would be awful. But it isn't. It's quite exciting. Only he doesn't speak much German. He's a Yugoslavian. That's why I don't know much about the picture. But I'm sure it will be all right. He'll write in something, and he's got ideas about South America later.

Why not? Oh, you mean brothels and things. Oh no, darling. I'll be terribly careful, I'll take references and everything. And now I've got to go. . . .

53

THE PUBLIC EYE
Peter Shaffer

Belinda, young, vivacious and unconventional, is talking to her husband Charles, a staid businessman. Three weeks before, she suddenly became aware that a man was following her around London. She describes the whole progress of her affair up to date. In fact, the man is a detective sent by an agency employed by Charles to watch her movements. Charles unjustly suspects her of infidelity.

BELINDA: All right. . . . First let me tell you the oddest thing about this whole affair. I call it an affair because it is one. Do you know, for the whole three weeks since we first saw each other, we haven't exchanged a single word? When I say we meet every day, I don't mean we make a date. All that happens is that everywhere I go he's sure to follow. Like Mary's little lamb. He's a pure genius at following. You never see him till he decides to show himself. Then he just pops up—click!—in a coffee-bar or a cinema, or out from behind a statue in the park. Once I turned round and there he was in the ladies' powder room at Fortnums. I suppose at the start I ought to have been scared, but I never was. Isn't that odd? I'd no idea what he wanted, and it didn't matter. Of course I realized he must be the loneliest man in town, but then in a way I was the loneliest girl, so it was sort of fitting. Who was I to complain if he got his kicks following me around? After a bit—and this is the really kooky thing—I began to get mine by following *him*.
CHARLES: What!
BELINDA: The day came when he took over. I'd stopped outside a cinema where there was a horror film, and I looked back as usual, just to make sure he'd seen me go in. And you know, he shook his head. He was not going to see that film. He was like you, you see; he didn't really like horror

films. Mind you he'd had a bit of a do with them; I'd made him sit through eleven that week. Instead he turned round, signed for me to follow and marched off to the next cinema. That was the first time I'd ever seen an Ingmar Bergman film. Charles, they're marvelous! This one has a poor old man driving all over Sweden in a motorcar, looking for the turning he took wrong years before. It's pathetic.

CHARLES: No doubt.

BELINDA: It is really. At one point he sees himself in his own coffin!

CHARLES: And this is all you've got to tell me.

BELINDA: Yes. Anyway as far as what you're thinking's concerned. After that the whole thing became wonderful. We never knew what each day would bring. Sometimes I'd lead, and sometimes he would. Last week I marched into the National Gallery and stopped in front of Bellini's *Portrait of a Doge*. He was terribly grateful; you know, he'd obviously never seen it! He paid me back by leading me out to Syon House, which is hidden away behind all sorts of slummy things in Isleworth, and has a huge hall of green marble, and eight statues in gold, life-size! I know everything about him, now, even what he likes to eat. They're all sweet things—he must be a Turk or something. Actually he dresses a bit Turkey. And he knows everything about me. One day we were in a shop and he laid out this—(*she picks up the sombrero*) for me to buy. And it's the only hat I don't look stupid in.

CHARLES: Thank you.

BELINDA: Oh, Charles, it's not a question of hats. I've had the most intimate relationship of my life with someone I've never spoken to. What does it mean? . . . When I'm with him I live.

Omit all Charles' lines and Belinda's "Yes. Anyway as far as what you're thinking's concerned."

A RESOUNDING TINKLE

N. F. Simpson

The play is set in a suburban living room. Middie and Bro Paradock appear to be a normal suburban couple until one hears their conversation. N. F. Simpson satirizes the life of the suburbs in this play. Here Middie is talking on the telephone to Mrs. Stencil who is passionately concerned with the welfare of eagles. It is essential that the actress playing Middie appears to be completely unaware of anything ridiculous in the lines.

MIDDIE: Mrs. Paradock . . . oh, Mrs. Stencil . . . yes. . . . No, Bro's just this moment gone out . . . yes . . . yes, yes, I can imagine . . . of course it is . . . of course . . . yes, . . .yes. . . . Oh, but I think they get used to it, Mrs. Stencil, don't they? They get a sort of head for heights. . . . I really don't think heights worry them, Mrs. Stencil. . . . Some birds, perhaps—but not eagles. . . . Oh, yes. Eagles do. . . . Yes. . . . But it must be very rare, however high they fly. . . . It must be very rare for an eagle to come over dizzy. . . . Yes, yes. . . . But wouldn't that give them the feeling of being rather hampered? Yes. . . . But I do think an eagle likes to swoop down sometimes. . . . But not if it's wearing a parachute. . . . Oh, I can understand how you feel, Mrs. Stencil. . . . Yes. . . . Yes. . . . (*Hesitantly*) I'm afraid it would have to be more or less a token subscription this time—this is always our expensive quarter . . . No, naturally. . . . No. . . . Anyway, I'll tell Bro when he comes in, and . . . yes . . . yes . . . I suppose they must. . . . It's the peering down most of the time. . . . And of course with some of them they're supposed to stare into the sun as well, aren't they? Don't eagles stare at the sun? Yes . . . still, I should think if they found that. . . . Yes. . . . But if they found . . . it was becoming a strain on their eyes they'd surely stop doing it. . . . Yes. . . . But I doubt whether they'd take the trouble to wear them once the novelty had worn off. . . . They are—they're very expensive. Even the steel-rimmed ones. . . . Yes. . . . A kind of welfare state for animals, in fact. . . . Yes—Well, I'll tell Bro, Mrs. Stencil, when he comes in and . . . yes. . . . Yes, I will, Mrs. Stencil. . . . Good-by. (*She replaces the receiver*)

THE RIVALS

R. B. Sheridan

The action of the play takes place on a summer's day in the fashionable Bath of the 1770s. Captain Absolute, heir to Sir Anthony Absolute, has assumed the name and rank of Ensign Beverley in order to woo Lydia Languish, Mrs. Malaprop's niece. Mrs. Malaprop has discovered the intrigue through an intercepted note and has confined Lydia to the house. In this scene, Mrs. Malaprop is talking to Sir Anthony, who she does not realize is "Beverley's" father. Sir Anthony has mentioned that he has seen Lydia's maid coming out of the circulating library with books for her mistress. He condemns libraries for spreading dangerous ideas and asks Mrs. Malaprop what she thinks a woman should know. Lydia's "old tough aunt" answers in a speech full of the malapropisms which have made her famous in literature.

MRS. MALAPROP: Observe me, Sir Anthony, I would by no means wish a daughter of mine to be a progeny of learning; I don't think so much learning becomes a young woman; for instance, I would never let her meddle with Greek, or Hebrew, or algebra, or simony or fluxions, or paradoxes, or such inflammatory branches of learning—neither would it be necessary for her to handle any of your mathematical, astronomical, diabolical instruments.—But, Sir Anthony, I would send her at nine years old to a boarding school, in order to learn a little ingenuity and artifice. Then, sir, she should have a supercilious knowledge in accounts,—and as she grew up, I would have her instructed in geometry, that she might know something of the contageous countries;—but above all, Sir Anthony, she should be mistress of orthodoxy that she might not misspell, and mispronounce words so shamefully as girls usually do; and likewise that she might reprehend the true meaning of what she is saying. This, Sir Anthony, is what I would have a woman know;—and I don't think there is a superstitious article in it.

THE WAY OF THE WORLD

William Congreve

The play is set in London in 1700. Lady Wishfort, a vigorous, lusty fifty-five, is the sworn enemy of Mirabell because he falsely pretended to love her. She now protests her dislike of men but is still pursuing them and drinking ratafia, a popular liqueur of the period, to give herself staying power. In this scene she is at her dressing table, railing at her servant Peg and waiting impatiently for her woman, Foible.

ACT III, SCENE i

LADY WISHFORT: Merciful, no news of Foible yet?

PEG: No, madam.

LADY WISHFORT: I have no more patience—if I have not fretted myself till I am pale again, there's no veracity in me. Fetch me the red—the red, do you hear, sweetheart? An errant ash color, as I'm a person. Look you how this wench stirs! Why dost thou not fetch me a little red? Didst thou not hear me, mopus?

PEG: The red ratafia does your ladyship mean, or the cherry-brandy?

LADY WISHFORT: Ratafia, fool. No, fool. Not the ratafia, fool—grant me patience! I mean the Spanish paper, idiot, complexion darling. Paint, paint, paint, dost thou understand that, changeling, dangling thy hands like bobbins before thee? Why dost thou not stir, puppet? thou wooden thing upon wires.

PEG: Lord, madam, your ladyship is so impatient—I cannot come at the paint, madam. Mrs. Foible has locked it up, and carried the key with her.

LADY WISHFORT: A pox take you both—fetch me the cherry brandy then.

SCENE ii

LADY WISHFORT: I'm as pale and as faint, I look like Mrs. Qualmsick the curate's wife, that's always breeding—wench, come. Come, wench, what art thou doing, sipping? Tasting? Save thee, dost thou not know the bottle?

SCENE iii

LADY WISHFORT, PEG *with a bottle and china cup.*

PEG: Madam, I was looking for a cup.

LADY WISHFORT: A cup, save thee, and what a cup hast thou brought! Dost thou take me for a fairy, to drink out of an acorn? Why didst thou not bring thy thimble? Hast thou ne'er a brass thimble clinking in thy pocket with a bit of nutmeg? I warrant thee. Come, fill, fill! So. Again. (*There is a knock at the door*) See who that is. Set down the bottle first—here, here under the table.

Omit all Peg's lines.

VERSE PLAYS

ANTONY AND CLEOPATRA
William Shakespeare

After the death of Antony, the victorious Caesar means to lead Cleopatra in triumph through Rome. She is taken prisoner at the Monument. While awaiting the arrival of Caesar she talks to her guard, Dolabella, about her dream that there was "an Emperor Antony." This is the final scene of the play; at the end of it Cleopatra kills herself, rather than submit to Caesar.

ACT V, SCENE ii

CLEOPATRA: You laugh when boys or women tell their
    dreams; is't not your trick?

DOLABELLA: I understand not, madam.

CLEOPATRA: I dreamt there was an Emperor Antony—
    O, such another sleep, that I might see
    But such another man!

DOLABELLA: If it might please ye—

CLEOPATRA: His face was as the heav'ns, and therein stuck
    A sun and moon, which kept their course and lighted
    The little O, the earth.

DOLABELLA: Most sovereign creature—

CLEOPATRA: His legs bestrid the ocean; his rear'd arm
    Crested the world. His voice was propertied
    As all the tuned spheres, and that to friends;

60

But when he meant to quail and shake the orb,
He was as rattling thunder. For his bounty,
There was no winter in't; an autumn 'twas
That grew the more by reaping. His delights
Were dolphin-like: they show'd his back above
The element they liv'd in. In his livery
Walk'd crowns and crownets; realms and islands were
As plates dropp'd from his pocket.
DOLABELLA: Cleopatra—
CLEOPATRA: Think you there was or might be such a man
  As this I dreamt of?

Omit all Dolabella's lines.

THE ASCENT OF F6
W. H. Auden and Christopher Isherwood

The play was written in 1936 and reflects the disillusionment
of the 1930s. A stage box is illuminated and in it Mrs. A, a
suburban housewife, is seen standing at her stove, cooking. Her
husband, Mr. A, enters at the end of the speech and takes up
her note of despair "nothing that matters will ever happen."
The scene ends with Mrs. A asking
          "Give us something to live for.
          We have waited too long."

ACT I, SCENE i
MRS. A: Evening. A slick and unctuous Time
  Has sold us yet another shop-soiled day,
  Patently rusty, not even in a gaudy box.
  I have dusted the six small rooms:

The parlour, once the magnificent image of my freedom
And the bedroom, which once held for me
The mysterious languors of Egypt and the terrifying
Indias.
The delivery vans have paid their brief impersonal visits.
I have eaten a scrappy lunch from a plate on my knee.
I have spoken with acquaintances in the Stores;
Under our treble gossip heard the menacing throb
of our hearts
As I hear them now, as all of us hear them,
Standing at our stoves in these villas, expecting our
husbands;
The drums of an enormous and routed army,
Throbbing raggedly, fitfully, scatteredly, madly.
We are lost. We are lost.

THE DUCHESS OF MALFI

John Webster

The play was published in 1623 and written about ten years
earlier. The setting is a north Italian ducal court. Earlier in the
play, the duchess, a young and beautiful widow, has married the
master of her household, Antonio, despite her two brothers'
objections. Their agent, Bosola, makes the duchess a prisoner
in her own castle and there her brother Ferdinand terrorizes
her with gruesome devices such as a dead man's hand, a procession of madmen and the artificial figures of Antonio and his
children "appearing as if they were dead."

In this scene Bosola and the executioners appear with bell,
coffin and strangling cords. Bosola is amazed by the serene way
in which she faces these terrors, even managing to make a grim

joke in her final speech. The opening lines of this scene are spoken to Cariola, her waiting woman.

ACT IV, Scene ii

DUCHESS: Farewell, Cariola.
>In my last will I have not much to give:
>A many hungry guests have fed upon me;
>Thine will be a poor reversion.

CARIOLA: I will die with her.

DUCHESS: I pray thee, look thou giv'st my little boy
>Some syrup for his cold, and let the girl
>Say her prayers ere she sleep
>
>(CARIOLA *is forced out by the executioners*)
>
>Now what you please:
>What death?

BOSOLA: Strangling; here are your executioners.

DUCHESS: I forgive them:
>The apoplexy, catarrh, or cough o' the lungs,
>Would do as much as they do.

BOSOLA: Doth not death fright you?

DUCHESS: Who would be afraid on't,
>Knowing to meet such excellent company
>In the other world?

BOSOLA: Yet, methinks,
>The manner of your death should much afflict you:
>This cord should terrify you.

DUCHESS: Not a whit:
>What would it pleasure me to have my throat cut
>With diamonds? or to be smotherèd
>With cassia? Or to be shot to death with pearls?
>I know death hath ten thousand several doors
>For men to take their exits; and 'tis found
>They go on such strange geometrical hinges,
>You may open them both ways; any way, for Heaven sake,
>So I were out of your whispering. Tell my brothers

That I perceive death, now I am well awake,
Best gift is they can give or I can take.
I would fain put off my last woman's fault,
I'd not be tedious to you.
FIRST EXECUTIONER: We are ready.
DUCHESS: Dispose my breath how please you; but my body
    Bestow upon my women, will you?
FIRST EXECUTIONER: Yes.
DUCHESS: Pull, and pull strongly, for your able strength
    Must pull down Heaven upon me:—
    Yet stay; Heaven-gates are not so highly arched
    As princes' palaces; they that enter there
    Must go upon their knees (*Kneels*)—Come, violent
    death,
    Serve for mandragora to make me sleep!—
    Go tell my brothers, when I am laid out,
    They then may feed in quiet.
(*The EXECUTIONERS strangle the DUCHESS*)

*Omit Cariola's line, Bosola's lines, the first executioner's lines
and the duchess's line "Not a whit."*

THE FIRST BORN

Christopher Fry

This play was written partly before and partly during the
Second World War. It is set in Egypt at the time of the
Pharaohs. In this speech Anath, a woman of fifty, sister to the
Pharaoh, is telling Moses' young "cousin" how, as a girl, she
found Moses in a cradle among the Nile bulrushes and how he
grew up at court, became a great warrior and finally recognized
his true ancestry.

ANATH: Yes, they all died of a signature. Or we thought so,
    Until the thirtieth of August. I went bathing on that day.
    I was a girl then, Teusret, and played with the Nile
    As though with a sister. And afterwards as I waded
    To land again, pushing the river with my knees,
    The wash rocked a little ark out
    Into the daylight: and in the ark I found
    A tiny weeping Israel who had failed
    To be exterminated. When I stooped
    With my hair dripping on to his face,
    He stopped in a screwed-up wail and looked.
    And when I found my hands and crowded him
    Into my breast, he buried like a burr.
    And when I spoke, I laughed, and when I laughed
    I cried, he was so enchanting. I was ready
    To raise a hornet's nest to keep him; in fact
    I raised one. All the court flew up and buzzed.
    But what could they do? Not even my Pharaoh-father
    Could sting him out of my arms. So he grew up
    Into your tall cousin, Egyptian
    From beard to boots and, what was almost better,
    A soldier of genius. You don't remember
    How I held you on this terrace, to see him come home
    from war?
    It was ten years ago. Do you remember
    The shrieking music, and half Egypt shouting
    Conqueror! Peacemaker!
TEUSRET: No.
ANATH: They have all tried to forget.
    They have blotted him out of the records, but not out
    Of my memory.

Omit Teusret's line.

KING HENRY IV, PART I

William Shakespeare

Henry IV and Henry Percy (Hotspur) have quarreled over the prisoners that Hotspur has taken in his battle against the Scots. Hotspur is furious because the king has refused to "ransom home revolted Mortimer." Now Hotspur and his uncle Worcester are plotting to rise against the king, uniting the powers of Scotland, York and Mortimer against him.

Hotspur, in this scene, has just received a letter refusing him support for his project. Fearful that the king will be informed of the situation, he decides to leave Warkworth Castle within two hours to set the plot in motion. In this speech, his spirited wife, sister to Mortimer, tries to find out what has been occupying his waking and sleeping thoughts for the last fortnight.

ACT II, SCENE iii

LADY PERCY: O, my good lord, why are you thus alone?
    For what offence have I this fortnight been
    A banish'd woman from my Harry's bed?
    Tell me, sweet lord, what is't that takes from thee
    Thy stomach, pleasure, and thy golden sleep?
    Why dost thou bend thine eyes upon the earth,
    And start so often when thou sitt'st alone?
    Why hast thou lost the fresh blood in thy cheeks,
    And given my treasures and my rights of thee
    To thick-ey'd musing and curs'd melancholy?
    In thy faint slumbers I by thee have watch'd,
    And heard thee murmur tales of iron wars;
    Speak terms of manage to thy bounding steed;
    Cry, Courage!—to the field!—and thou hast talk'd
    Of sallies and retires, of trenches, tents,
    Of palisadoes, frontiers, parapets,
    Of basilisks, of cannon, culverin,
    Of prisoners' ransom, and of soldiers slain,
    And all the currents of a heady fight.

Thy spirit within thee hath been so at war,
And thus hath so bestirr'd thee in thy sleep
That beads of sweat have stood upon thy brow,
Like bubbles in a late disturbed stream;
And in thy face strange motions have appear'd,
Such as we see when men restrain their breath
On some great sudden hest. O, what portents are these?
Some heavy business hath my lord in hand,
And I must know it, else he loves me not.

KING HENRY VI, PART I
William Shakespeare

After the death of Henry V, France has revolted against English
domination, Talbot has been defeated by the French and the
Dauphin, Charles, has been crowned king at Rheims. The
English, however, continue to hold out at Orleans. In this scene,
the Bastard of Orleans brings Joan of Arc—La Pucelle—to
Charles. She has had a vision in which she has been told that
she is destined to raise the siege and to drive the English out of
France. Reignier, Duke of Anjou, pretends to be Charles, but
when Joan comes in, she realizes the deception, recognizes
Charles and calls him forward, addressing her speech to him.

ACT I, SCENE ii
LA PUCELLE: Dauphin, I am by birth a shepherd's
daughter
My wit untrain'd in any kind of art.
Heaven and our Lady gracious hath it pleas'd
To shine on my contemptible estate:
Lo, whilst I waited on my tender lambs,

And to sun's parching heat display'd my cheeks,
God's Mother deigned to appear to me,
And in a vision full of majesty
Will'd me to leave my base vocation,
And free my country from calamity:
Her aid she promis'd and assur'd success:
In complete glory she reveal'd herself;
And whereas I was black with swart before,
With those clear rays which she infus'd on me,
That beauty am I bless'd with which you see.
Ask me what question thou canst possible,
And I will answer unpremeditated:
My courage, try by combat if thou dar'st.
And thou shalt find that I exceed my sex.
Resolve on this,—thou shalt be fortunate
If thou receive me for thy warlike mate.

KING HENRY VI, PART III

William Shakespeare

Margaret of Anjou, Henry VI's queen, furious because he has put aside his son's right to the succession in favor of Richard Plantagenet, Duke of York, has taken the field against York and, in this battlefield speech, she is taunting him with references to his son, Rutland, whom Clifford has killed.

ACT I, SCENE iv

QUEEN MARGARET: Brave warriors, Clifford and North-
    umberland,
    Come, make him stand upon this molehill here,
    That raught at mountains with outstretched arms,

Yet parted but the shadow with his hand.—
What, was it you that would be England's king?
Was't you that revell'd in our parliament,
And made a preachment of your high descent?
Where are your mess of sons to back you now?
The wanton Edward and the lusty George?
And where's that valiant crook-back prodigy,
Dicky your boy, that with his grumbling voice
Was wont to cheer his dad in mutinies?
Or, with the rest, where is your darling Rutland?
Look, York: I stain'd this napkin with the blood
That valiant Clifford, with his rapier's point,
Made issue from the bosom of the boy;
And if thine eyes can water for his death,
I give thee this to dry thy cheeks withal.
Alas, poor York! But that I hate thee deadly,
I should lament thy miserable state.
I pr'ythee, grieve to make me merry, York.
What hath thy fiery heart so parch'd thine entrails
That not a tear can fall for Rutland's death?
Why art thou patient, man? thou shouldst be made;
And I, to make thee mad, do mock thee thus.
Stamp, rave, and fret, that I may sing and dance.
Thou wouldst be fee'd, I see, to make me sport;
York cannot speak unless he wear a crown.—
A crown for York!—and, lords, bow low to him;—
Hold you his hands whilst I do set it on.
(*Putting a paper crown on his head*)
    Ay, marry, sir, now looks he like a king!
Ay, this is he that took King Henry's chair;
And this is he was his adopted heir.—
But how is it that great Plantagenet
Is crown'd so soon, and broke his solemn oath?
As I bethink me, you should not be king
Till our King Henry had shook hands with death.

And will you pale your head in Henry's glory,
And rob his temples of the diadem
Now in his life, against your holy oath?
O, 'tis a fault too, too, unpardonable!—
Off with the crown; and, with the crown, his head;
And whilst we breathe take time to do him dead.

A PHOENIX TOO FREQUENT
Christopher Fry

The scene is the tomb of Virilius, near Ephesus. Dynamene, his widow, has been keeping vigil by her husband's bier and has now fallen asleep. Doto, her maid, is talking to herself in the darkness. The play has been described as a *jeu d'esprit* about classical times.

An underground tomb, in darkness except for the very low light of an oil lamp. Above ground the starlight shows a line of trees on which hang the bodies of several men. It also penetrates a gate and falls onto the first of the steps which descend into the darkness of the tomb. DOTO talks to herself in the dark.

DOTO: Nothing but the harmless day gone into black
    Is all the dark is. And so what's my trouble?
    Demons is so much wind. Are so much wind.
    I've plenty to fill my thoughts. All that I ask
    Is don't keep turning men over in my mind,
    Venerable Aphrodite. I've had my last one
    And thank you. I thank thee. He smelt of sour grass
    And was likable. He collected ebony quoits.
(*An owl hoots near at hand*)
    O Zeus! O some god or other, where is the oil?

Fire's from Prometheus. I thank thee. If I
Mean to die I'd better see what I'm doing.
(*She fills the lamp with oil. The flame burns up brightly and
shows DYNAMENE, beautiful and young, leaning
asleep beside a bier*)
Honestly, I would rather have to sleep
With a bald bee-keeper who was wearing his boots
Than spend more days fasting and thirsting and crying
In a tomb. I shouldn't have said that. Pretend
I didn't hear myself. But life and death
Is cat and dog in this double-bed of a world.
My master, my poor master, was a man
Whose nose was as straight as a little buttress,
And now he has taken it into Elysium
Where it won't be noticed among all the other straight-
ness.
(*The owl cries again and wakens DYNAMENE*)
Oh, them owls. Those owls. It's woken her.

TROILUS AND CRESSIDA

William Shakespeare

The scene is Pandarus' orchard, Troy at the time of the Trojan
Wars. Troilus, son of Priam, King of Troy, is in love with
Cressida. Pandarus, her uncle, has been their go-between. Cressida has feigned reluctance but is attracted by Troilus. In a
soliloquy earlier in the play she has said

"Then though my heart's content firm love doth bear,
Nothing of that shall from mine eyes appear."

In this scene she is painting a picture of maidenly modesty
as she bashfully confesses her love, which hardly matches the

71

picture we have seen of her in her conversation with Pandarus in Act I.

ACT III, SCENE ii

CRESSIDA: Boldness comes to me now, and brings me
    heart:—
    Prince Troilus, I have lov'd you night and day
    For many weary months.
TROILUS: Why was my Cressid, then, so hard to win?
CRESSIDA: Hard to seem won; but I was won, my lord,
    With the first glance that ever—pardon me—
    If I confess much, you will play the tyrant.
    I love you now; but not, till now, so much
    But I might master it: in faith, I lie;
    My thoughts were like unbridl'd children, grown
    Too headstrong for their mother:—see, we fools!
    Why have I blabb'd? who shall be true to us,
    When we are so unsecret to ourselves?—
    But, though I lov'd you well, I woo'd you not;
    And yet, good faith, I wish'd myself a man,
    Or that we women had men's privilege
    Of speaking first. Sweet, bid me hold my tongue;
    For, in this rapture, I shall surely speak
    The thing I shall repent. See, see, your silence,
    Cunning in dumbness, from my weakness draws
    My very soul of conscience!—Stop my mouth.
TROILUS: And shall, albeit sweet music issues thence.
PANDARUS: Pretty, i' faith.
CRESSIDA: My lord, I do beseech you, pardon me;
    'Twas not my purpose thus to beg a kiss:
    I am asham'd;—O heavens! what have I done?
    For this time will I take my leave, my lord.
TROILUS: Your leave, sweet Cressid!
PANDARUS: Leave! An you take leave till tomorrow
    morning,—

CRESSIDA: Pray you, content you.

TROILUS: What offends you, lady?

CRESSIDA: Sir, mine own company.

TROILUS: You cannot shun
　　Yourself.

CRESSIDA: Let me go and try:
　　I have a kind of self resides with you;
　　But an unkind self, that itself will leave
　　To be another's fool. I would be gone:—
　　Where is my wit? I know not what I speak.

TROILUS: Well know they what they speak that speak so
　　wisely.

CRESSIDA: Perchance, my lord, I show more craft than
　　love;
　　And fell so roundly to a large confession,
　　To angle for your thoughts: but you are wise;
　　Or else you love not; for to be wise and love
　　Exceeds man's might; that dwells with gods above.

*Omit Cressida's "Sir, mine own company" and, "Let me go
and try" and all Troilus' and Pandarus' lines.*

THE WAKEFIELD MYSTERY PLAYS

edited by Martial Rose

This speech is taken from *The Crucifixion*, one of the plays in
the Wakefield Cycle of Mystery Plays. In this scene Jesus is
nailed to the cross. There is protracted dialogue and stage business from the four torturers as Jesus is stretched on the cross,
which is then raised. Mary enters and sees her son.

MARY: Alas! For care I cry, and stagger in my need!
Why hangst thou, son, so high? My ills begin to breed.
All blemished is thy beauty, I see thy body bleed!
In world, son, had we never such ill fate decreed.

My flesh that I have fed,
In life lovingly led,
Full straitly art thou stead
   Among thy foemen fell;
Such sorrow for to see,
My dearest child on thee,
Is more pain to me
Than any tongue can tell.

Alas, thy holy head
Without rest is revealed;
Thy face, with blood now red,
   Was fair as flower in field;
Who may not stand in dread
To see her bairn thus bled,
Beaten blue as lead,
   And have no limb to wield!

Fastened by hands and feet
With nails that his flesh eat,
With wounds his foes him greet,
   Alas, my child for care!
   Thy flesh is open wide
I see on either side
Tears of blood down glide
   Over all thy body bare.
Alas that I should bide
To see my son thus fare!

THE ZEAL OF THY HOUSE

Dorothy Sayers

The play is set in the Middle Ages between 1175 and 1179. The Lady Ursula de Warbois, widow of a wealthy knight, has come to live in Canterbury. In this scene she is talking to William of Sens, who designed and built the greater part of Canterbury Cathedral. In the speech preceding this one of Lady Ursula's he has said

"Your old men shall dream dreams
And your young men see visions but not your women."

This is her reply.

PART II

URSULA: I understand.
      Knowledge and work—knowledge is given to man
      And not to woman; and the glory of work
      To man and not to woman. But by whom
      Came either work or knowledge into the world?
      Not by the man. God said, "Ye shall not know;
      Knowledge is death." And Adam was afraid.
      But Eve, careless of peril, careless of death.
      Hearing the promise, "Ye shall be as gods,"
      Seized knowledge for herself, and for the man,
      And all the sons of men; knowledge, like God;
      Power to create, like God; and, unlike God,
      Courage to die. And the reward for her
      Was sorrow; but for Adam the reward
      Was work—of which he now contrives to boast
      As his particular glory, and in one breath
      Denies it to the woman and blames her for it,
      Winning the toss both ways. My simple Adam,
      It is too late to scare woman with risks
      And perils—woman, that for one splendid risk

75

Changed the security of Paradise,
Broke up the loom and pattern of creation,
Let in man's dream on the world, and snatched the torch
Of knowledge from the jealous hand of God
So that the fire runs in man's blood for ever.

Part Two

SPEECHES
FOR MEN

DRAMATIC SPEECHES

THE AFFAIR
Ronald Millar from the novel by C. P. Snow

The Affair was dramatized by Ronald Millar from the novel by Lord Snow. The play is set in the present in a Cambridge college during a Court of Sessions. This particular speech is the climax of the scene and provided an electrifying moment in the theater in the original production.

The court is sitting to reconsider the case of Dr. Howard who has recently been deprived of his fellowship because of a supposed scientific fraud in his thesis. Howard is aggressively anti-establishment and represents the younger generation of "new men" at the university. Sir Lewis Eliot, M.B.E., M.A., a former fellow of the college, has come down to defend Howard and to ensure that Howard's unattractive personality is not allowed to affect the verdict. Eliot is particularly disturbed by the attitude of Nightingale, the bursar, as revealed in a conversation he has had with him earlier.

NIGHTINGALE: We should never have elected such a man. Never, never, never!

LEWIS: Why? Because he believes what he believes? Because he thinks what he thinks?

NIGHTINGALE: Because he is *what* he is.

There is the strongest possible contrast of personality between Eliot, who has been a don, a barrister, an is now a senior civil servant, and Howard. Eliot succeeds in getting Dr. Howard's fellowship restored, but at the end of the play Eliot and the counsel representing the court have a short scene in which Eliot reveals that he has not achieved peace of mind despite the success he has just gained in the court.

LEWIS (*rising*): Master, like my colleague, I do not intend to recapitulate what the court has heard so often. But, with respect, I suggest to the court that today it has heard not one, but two pieces of critical testimony—Sir Francis Getliffe's— and the bursar's. The bursar did not speculate. He made a categorical and quite uncompromising statement, not only that in his view Dr. Howard should never have been elected a fellow of this college, but that, and I quote: "He ought to be got rid of." He gave his reasons, deeply felt, highly emotional reasons. Master, making up names for what we do not like and cannot bother to examine carefully is a common and dangerous pastime. We all know scientists whose politics are the same as Howard's and whose integrity is absolute. And yet this court has heard the view expressed—and violently expressed by one of its own members—that character and belief go hand in hand. Isn't this nonsense and dangerous nonsense? (*With mounting force and passion*) Isn't it the chronic danger, the madness of our time, for the world outside this college to divide into two halves? For each half to be blacked out and blinded by a fog of prejudice so thick that people on the two sides are ceasing to think of each other as belonging to the same species? Hasn't this fog, this murderous lunatic fog of prejudice, which is daily suffocating man's natural tolerance and understanding of his brother man, seeped inside these college walls and obscured this case from the beginning? Isn't *that* the heart, the *crux* of this whole affair? In the name of justice, in the name of tolerance, in the name of *survival*, I ask the court to revoke its decision, and declare Howard innocent. (*He resumes his seat.*)

CAMINO REAL

Tennessee Williams

The play is set on the plaza of what looks like a tropical seaport. From it a great flight of stairs leads through an arch to Terra Incognita—a wasteland which stretches from the walled town to the far mountains. In this town are gathered various characters who have died, famous names from literature, such as Marguerite Gautier, and also modern personalities such as the American champ boxer Kilroy. As Marguerite says, "We're threatened with eviction for this is a port of entry and departure, there are no permanent guests!" These souls are awaiting the next stage of their journey.

In this scene Lord Byron has just described to Marguerite and to Casanova the burning of Shelley's drowned corpse on the beach at Viareggio and how the poet's friend Trelawney snatched the heart of the body away from the flames.

"I thought it was a disgusting thing to do, to snatch a man's heart from his body. What can one man do with another man's heart?" he asks. Jacques Casanova seizes a loaf of bread from the table and demonstrates with it how one man can twist, tear, stamp on and kick another man's heart.

It is at this point that Lord Byron limps forward on to the stage apron and addresses the audience directly in the following speech. After it, he makes his exit through the arch to the desert of Terra Incognita.

BLOCK EIGHT

Lord Byron turns away from him and limps again out upon the stage apron and speaks to the audience.

BYRON: That's very true, Señor. But a poet's vocation, which used to be my vocation, is to influence the heart in a gentler fashion than you have made your mark on that loaf of bread. He ought to purify it and lift it above its ordinary level. For what is the heart but a sort of—(*He makes a high, groping gesture in the air*)—A sort of—*instrument!*—that translates noise into music, chaos into—*order* . . . (*Abdullah*

81

ducks almost to the earth in an effort to stifle his mirth;
Gutman coughs to cover his own amusement)—a mysterious
order!

(*He raises his voice till it fills the plaza*)
—That was my vocation once upon a time, before it was
obscured by vulgar plaudits!
—Little by little it was lost among gondolas and palazzos!—
masked balls, glittering salons, huge shadowy courts and
torch-lit entrances!—Baroque façades, canopies and carpets,
candelabra and gold plate among snowy damask, ladies with
throats as slender as flower-stems, bending and breathing
toward me their fragrant breath—
—Exposing their breasts to me!

Whispering, half-smiling!—And everywhere marble, the
visible grandeur of marble, pink and gray marble, veined
and tinted as flayed corrupting flesh—all these provided
agreeable distractions from the rather frightening solitude of
a poet. Oh, I wrote many cantos in Venice and Constanti-
nople and in Ravenna and Rome on all of those Latin and
Levantine excursions that my twisted foot led me into but I
wonder about them a little. They seem to improve as the
wine in the bottle—dwindles . . . *There is a passion for*
declivity in this world!

And lately I've found myself listening to hired musicians
behind a row of artificial palm trees—instead of the single—
pure-stringed instrument of my heart . . .

Well, then, it's time to leave here!

(*He turns back to the stage*)

There is a time for departure even when there's no certain
place to go!

I'm going to look for one, now. I'm sailing to Athens. At
least I can look up at the Acropolis, I can stand at the foot of
it and look up at broken columns on the crest of a hill—if not
purity, at least its recollection . . .

82

I can sit quietly looking for a long, long time in absolute
silence, and possibly, yes *still* possibly—

The old pure music will come to me again. Of course on
the other hand I may hear only the little noise of insects
in the grass . . .

But I am sailing to Athens! *Make voyages!—Attempt
them!*—there's nothing else . . .

THE CARETAKER
Harold Pinter

This is the most famous speech from *The Caretaker* and if
played correctly, can produce a tremendous impact. There are
three characters in the play, Aston and his brother Mick and
an old tramp, Davies. Two years before, Aston has had electrical
shock treatment in a mental home and this has left him numbed
and withdrawn from the world. He lives in his one room and
has been collecting materials to build a shed in the garden but
has never summoned up enough interest to start work on it.
His meeting with the tramp is the first thing that has re-awoken
his interest in life. In this speech he explains his experiences to
Davies. It is essential that the lines are spoken flatly and un-
emotionally. If the overtones of "I've often thought of going
back and trying to find the man who did that to me" are conveyed subtly, a real shock of horror will be produced on an
audience.

ACT II

ASTON: . . . About a week later they started to come round
and do this thing to the brain. We were all supposed to have
it done, in this ward. And they came round and did it one

83

at a time. One a night. I was one of the last. And I could see quite clearly what they did to the others. They used to come round with these . . . I don't know what they were . . . they looked like big pincers, with wires on, the wires were attached to a little machine. It was electric. They used to hold the man down, and this chief—the chief doctor, used to fit the pincers, something like earphones, he used to fit them on either side of the man's skull. There was a man holding the machine, you see, and he'd . . . he'd do something. . . . I can't remember now whether he pressed a switch or turned something, just a matter of switching the current . . . I suppose it was, and the chief would just press these pincers on either side of the skull and keep them there. Then he'd take them off. They'd cover the man up . . . and they wouldn't touch him again until later on. Some used to put up a fight, but most of them didn't. They just lay there. Well, they were coming round to me, and the night they came I got up and stood against the wall. They told me to get on the bed, and I knew they had to get me on the bed because if they did it while I was standing up they might break my spine. So I stood up and then one or two of them came for me, well, I was younger then, I was much stronger than I am now, I was quite strong then, I laid one of them out and I had another one round the throat, and then suddenly this chief had these pincers on my skull and I knew he wasn't supposed to do it while I was standing up, that's why I . . . anyway, he did it. So I did get out of the place . . . but I couldn't walk very well. I don't think my spine was damaged. That was perfectly all right. The trouble was . . . my thoughts . . . had become very slow . . . I couldn't think at all . . . I couldn't . . . get . . . my thoughts . . . together . . . uuuh . . . I could . . . never quite get it . . . together. The trouble was, I couldn't hear what people were saying. I couldn't look to the right or the left, I had to look straight in front of me, because if I turned my head round . . . I couldn't keep . . . upright. And I had these headaches. Then I went along to people, but they wanted to take me in, but I wasn't going to go in . . . anywhere. So I couldn't do any work, because I . . . I couldn't write any more, you see. I couldn't write my name. I used to sit in my room. That was when I lived with my mother. And my brother. He was younger than me. And I laid everything out, in order, in my room, all the things I knew were mine, but I didn't die. I never had those hallucinations any more. And I never spoke to anyone any more. The funny thing is, I can't remember much . . . about what I said, what I thought . . . I mean before I went into that place. The thing is, I should have been dead. I should have died. And then, anyway, after a time, I got a bit better, and I started to do things with my hands, and then about two years ago I came here, because my brother had got this house, and so I decided to have a go at decorating it, so I came into this room, and I started to collect wood, for my shed, and all these bits and pieces, that I thought might come in handy for the flat, or around the house, sometime. I feel much better now. But I don't talk to people now. I steer clear of places like that café. I never go into them now. I don't talk to anyone . . . like that. I've often thought of going back and trying to find the man who did that to me. But I want to do something first. I want to build that shed out in the garden.

THE DEVILS

John Whiting

The action of the play takes place in and near the town of Loudun in France between the years 1623 and 1634. Sister Jeanne-des-Anges, Mother Superior of the nunnery at Loudun, asks Grandier, the local priest and vicar of St. Peter's Church, to become the spiritual adviser to the order. Grandier is a brilliant preacher, a scholar and also a libertine; when he rejects her offer she accuses him of filling the nuns' minds with lust, working through the power of Satan. The following scene occurs before Grandier is brought to trial on a charge of diabolism. He is talking to the sewerman of the town.

Grandier is a man of thirty-five, a combination of intellectual force and sensualism.

ACT II

GRANDIER: I came out of the house. I thought I'd walk back, air myself after the death cell. I was very tired. I could hear Saint Peter's bell.

The road was dusty. I remembered the day I came here. I was wearing new shoes. They were white with dust. Do you know, I flicked them over with my stole before being received by the bishop. I was vain and foolish, then. Ambitious, too.

I walked on. They were working in the fields and called to me. I remembered how I loved to work with my hands when I was a boy. But my father said it was unsuitable for one of my birth. I could see my church in the distance. I was very proud, in a humble way. I thought of my love for the beauty of this not very beautiful place. And I remembered night in the building, with the gold, lit by candlelight, against the darkness. I thought of you. I remembered you as a friend.

I rested. The country was stretched out. Do you know where the rivers join?

I once made love there.

Children came past me. Yes, of course, that's where I got the flowers. I didn't pick them. They were given to me.

I watched the children go. Yes, I was very tired. I could see far beyond the point my eyes could see. Castles, cities, mountains, oceans, plains, forests—and—And then—oh, my son, my son—and then—I want to tell you—

SEWERMAN: Do so. Be calm.

GRANDIER: My son, I—Am I mad?

SEWERMAN: No. Quite sane. Tell me. What did you do?

GRANDIER: I created God!

(*Silence.*)

GRANDIER: I created Him from the light and the air, from the dust of the road, from the sweat of my hands, from gold, from filth, from the memory of women's faces, from great rivers, from children, from the works of man, from the past, the present, the future and the unknown. I caused Him to be from fear and despair. I gathered in everything from this mighty act, all I have known, seen and experienced. My sin, my presumption, my vanity, my love, my hate, my lust.

And last I gave myself and so made God. And He was magnificent. For He is all these things.

I was utterly in His presence. I knelt by the road. I took out the bread and the wine. *Panem vinum in salutis consecramus hostiam.* And in this understanding He gave Himself humbly and faithfully to me, as I had given myself to Him.

Omit the sewerman's lines.

EPITAPH FOR GEORGE DILLON
John Osborne

This play was written before *Look Back in Anger,* although it was staged after it, and George precedes Jimmie Porter as an angry young man. The scene is the home of the Elliotts, who have befriended George—an unsuccessful writer and actor. He is sponging on them while he is out of work. He is able to do this more easily because he reminds Mrs. Elliott of her dead son and he can get round Josie, the daughter, with what John Osborne describes as his "antiromantic kind of charm." However Mrs. Elliott's sister, Ruth, does not capitulate to him and in this scene in Act II each strips the other of illusions and George confesses to Ruth that his talent may not be a genuine one. When she asks him "Why are you so morbidly self-conscious? I thought all actors reveled in self-exhibitionism," George replies "Don't you believe it" and goes on to tell her in the following speech of an incident which happened to him when he was in the R.A.F. At the end of it she tells him that he is play-acting.

John Osborne describes George as a little over thirty with a boyish manner. "He displays at different times a mercurial, ironic passion, lethargy, offensiveness, blatant sincerity and a mentally picaresque dishonesty—sometimes all of these at the same time. A walking confliction in fact!"

ACT II

GEORGE: The one thing I never shoot lines about is the R.A.F. Just a gap in my life. That's all. Well, it happened like this: It was one night in particular, when it wasn't my turn to go on ops. Instead, we got a basinful of what we gave the Jerries, smack bang in the middle of the camp. I remember flinging myself down, not so much onto the earth as into it. A Wing Commander type pitched himself next to me, and together, we shared his tin helmet. Fear ran through the whole of my body, the strange fear that my right leg would be blown off, and how terrible it would be. Suddenly, the winco shouted at me above the din, "What's your profession?" "Actor," I said. The moment I uttered that word, machine-gun fire and bombs all around us, the name of my calling, my whole reason for existence—it sounded so hideously trivial and unimportant, so divorced from the living, and the real world, that my fear vanished. All I could feel was shame. (*He is lost for a moment or two. Then he adds brightly*)

Gifted people are always dramatizing themselves. It provides its own experience, I suppose.

LOOK BACK IN ANGER

John Osborne

When this play exploded into the West End in 1956, people heard for the first time in the theater the voice of the 1950s, of a disillusioned postwar generation. Jimmy Porter became the mouthpiece of its angry young men and the label has stuck to him ever since.

Jimmy is resentful because he feels that there are no great causes left to fight for and that the world as it exists is all wrong, but he is anxious to give as well as to demand and is bitter because no one, not even his wife, seems interested enough to take what he has to offer. Osborne has a great gift for rhetoric and Jimmy's long speeches generate fire in performance and succeed in making an audience feel strong emotions either for or against him.

Jimmy lives with Alison, his upper middle-class wife (he cannot forgive her for this) in a shabby attic in a town in the Midlands. Although he is a graduate, he makes his living by keeping a market sweet stall. He is constantly trying to force some reaction out of Alison, who has by now learned to take refuge behind an apparently impassive front. In this particular scene he is goading her in front of Cliff, who shares the attic with them, and Helen, Alison's repertory actress friend.

ACT II, SCENE i

JIMMY: The funny thing is, you know, I really did have to ride up on a white charger—off-white, really. Mummy locked her up in their eight-bedroomed castle, didn't she. There is no limit to what the middle-class mummy will do in the holy crusade against ruffians like me. Mummy and I took one quick look at each other, and, from then on, the age of chivalry was dead. I knew that, to protect her innocent young, she wouldn't hesitate to cheat, lie, bully and black-mail. Threatened with me, a young man without money, background or even looks, she'd bellow like a rhinoceros in labor—enough to make every male rhino for miles turn white, and pledge himself to celibacy. But even I underestimated her strength. Mummy may look over-fed and a bit flabby on the outside, but don't let that well-bred guzzler fool you. Underneath all that, she's armor-plated—She's as rough as a night in a Bombay brothel, and as tough as a matelot's arm. She's probably in that bloody cistern, taking down every word we say. (*Kicks cistern*) Can you 'ear me, mother. (*Sits on it, beats like bongo drums*) Just about get her in there. Let me give you an example of this lady's tactics. You may have noticed that I happen to wear my hair rather long. Now, if my wife is honest, or concerned enough to explain, she could tell you that this is not due to any dark, unnatural instincts I possess, but because (*a*) I can usually think of better things than a haircut to spend two bob on, and (*b*) I prefer long hair. But obvious, innocent explanation didn't appeal to Mummy at all: So she hires detectives to watch me, to see if she can't somehow get me into the *News of the World*. All so that I shan't carry off her daughter on that poor, old charger of mine, all tricked out and caparisoned in

90

discredited passions and ideals! The old gray mare that actually once led the charge against the old order—well, she certainly ain't what she used to be. It was all she could do to carry me, but your weight was too much for her. She just dropped dead on the way.

LUTHER
John Osborne

When writing this play, John Osborne used Martin Luther's own words whenever possible. Luther, the Protestant monk who had the courage to defy the hypocrisy that stemmed from the Vatican, is obsessed with the sense of his sinfulness. He is deeply concerned about his relationship with his father and mother and morbidly preoccupied with his own ill-health. Luther has attacked the practice and abuse of the sale of indulgences by the clergy to a credulous public, and has received a Bull threatening him with excommunication if he persists in defying the Church.

At the time of this speech he is thirty-seven and a distinguished member of the University of Wittenberg. It is the year before the Diet of Worms. The scene is evening at the Elster Gate, Wittenberg. The Bull issued against Luther appears as a back-cloth—above it a fish-head and bones. Monks come to and fro and hurl books of canon law, the papal decretals, onto the fire burning round the gate offstage. We can see the reflection of the flames rising round the gate. Martin comes in and ascends the pulpit.

ACT II, SCENE vi

MARTIN: I have been served with a piece of paper. Let me tell you about it. It has come to me from a latrine called Rome, the capital of the devil's own sweet empire. It is called the papal bull and it claims to excommunicate me, Dr. Martin Luther. These lies they raise up from paper like fumes from the bog of Europe; because papal decretals are the devil's excretals. I'll hold it up for you to see properly. You see the signature? Signed beneath the seal of the Fisherman's Ring by one certain midden cock called Leo, an overindulged Jake's attendant to Satan himself, a glittering worm in excrement, known to you as his holiness the pope. You may know him as the head of the church. Which he may still be: like a fish is the head of a cat's dinner: eyes without sight clutched to a stick of sucked bones. God has told me; there can be no dealings between this cat's dinner and me. And, as for this bull, it's going to roast, it's going to roast and so are the balls of the Medici! (*He descends and casts the bull into the flames. He begins to shake, as if he were unable to breathe; as if he were about to have another fit. Shaking, he kneels*)

Oh, God! Oh, God! Oh, thou my God, my God, help me against the reason and wisdom of the world. You must—there's only you—to do it. Breathe into me. Breathe into me like a lion into the mouth of a stillborn cub. This cause is not mine but yours. For myself, I've no business to be dealing with the great lords of this world. I want to be still, in peace, and alone. Breathe into me, Jesus. I rely on no man, only you. My God, my God, do you hear me? Are you dead? Are you dead? No, you can only hide yourself, can't you? Lord, I'm afraid. I am a child, the lost body of a child. I am stillborn.

Breathe into me, in the name of thy son, Jesus Christ, who shall be my protector and defender, yes, my mighty fortress, breathe into me.

MURDER MISTAKEN

Janet Greene

Edward Bare, a young estate agent's clerk, has murdered his wife, Monica, for her money. A visitor calling herself Charlotte arrives at the house. She subsequently turns out to be the murdered woman's sister, Dora. In this scene she has become convinced that Edward murdered Monica. She has made enquiries about his early life and has discovered a series of crimes which have never been pinned on him. Now, at the climax of the play, she confronts him with what she has found out and says "Look at you. Even if you escape the law, which isn't likely, you can never"—Edward suddenly throws up his arms and half shouts, half recites the end of her sentence—"I can never escape myself."

Although he starts the speech emotionally, by the end of it he is speaking in matter of fact, simple tones. On the words "That's why I'm going to kill you" he picks up the poker and advances on her, trying to force her to run.

She tells him that he is undergoing a paranoic tremor because she is standing her ground and manages to prevent him from attacking her. The playwright describes Edward as "handsome, smart, astute, very smooth. He has learned to control his accent but might drop an *h* when moved."

ACT II, SCENE iii

EDWARD: I can never escape myself. (*Rises*) I think I'm a sort of little Napoleon or something, but really I'm just the victim of a psychosis. (*To fireplace. He laughs and laughs*) I could give you the lines, Dora. Rotten social conditions comes next; the psycho routine. (*Turns to her*) I couldn't believe my ears when you started. Nearly laughed in your face. I've had the full treatment, Dora. The lot! And I never met an M.O. yet I didn't beat at his own game. Highly strung, imaginative, sensitive, emotional, but I always walked out with a clean bill of health. There's not one official mark against me, Dora. Now let me tell you what it's really like;

93

by one that's tried. (*In matter of fact, simple tones*) A man doesn't kill because some dappy old girl told him he was entitled to wear a coronet. If he's got any sense he checks up, when he's old enough to ask questions. He doesn't kill because he was in love with his mother, afraid of the man next door and saw his father go down the passage to his sister's room. He kills for one of two reasons; lust or money. In my case it's been money. Little Acton Bobby's Saturday six-pence, Aunty's seventy quid that I thought was seven hundred; and Monnie's money that I lost. I mean to have it, Dora. That's why I'm going to kill you.

RHINOCEROS
Eugene Ionesco

The play is set in the present, in a small French provincial town. As people are sitting at their tables in the square one Sunday in the summer, a rhinoceros races by; later, this phenomenon is repeated. Next day at the office, Berenger and his friend Daisy discover that one of their colleagues has turned into a rhinoceros. Gradually, more and more people join the herd, some willingly, some reluctantly. The more people join, the more the pressure is increased on the rest to conform as they are terrified of being thought different in any way from their fellows. Soon the rhinoceroses are the majority section of the population.

Berenger, a lazy, procrastinating kind of man, and Daisy are eventually the only human beings left in their own form. He resolves not to give in, not to follow the herd. When Daisy leaves him to become a rhinoceros Berenger is alone, an individualist against the mass.

The speech given here ends the play. Berenger is alone in his room. For a moment or two he thinks that perhaps he would

like to lose his human body, which has now become strange and
ugly to him because it is different from everyone else's, and to
change it for the hard, rough "wonderful dull green" skin of the
rhinoceroses. He thinks that he would like to trumpet in their
charming, if raucous, notes. But at the end of the speech he
suddenly snaps out of this mood, and regains his strength and
independence as he declares, "I'm the last man left, and I'm
staying that way until the end. I'm not capitulating."

ACT III

Daisy exits slowly L. The rhinoceros noises fade.
BERENGER (*still looking at himself in the mirror*): Men
aren't so bad-looking, you know. And I'm not a particularly
handsome specimen. Believe me, Daisy. (*He turns*) Daisy!
Daisy! (*He moves and looks off R*) Where are you, Daisy?
You can't do that to me. (*He darts to the door L and calls*)
Daisy! Daisy! Come back! Come back! my dear. You haven't
even had your lunch. Daisy, don't leave me alone. Remember your promise. Daisy! Daisy! (*He makes a despairing
gesture and crosses to C*) Well, it was obvious we weren't
getting along together. The home was broken up. It just
wasn't working out. But she shouldn't have left like that with
no explanation. (*He looks all around*) She didn't even leave
a message. That's no way to behave. (*He pauses*) Now I'm
all on my own. (*He bundles everything off the table C on to
the floor. Angrily*) But they won't get me. (*He carefully
closes the windows*) You won't get me. (*He moves the table
C and wedges it against the door L. He addresses all the
rhinoceroses*) I'm not joining you; I don't understand you.
(*He piles two chairs against the table*) I'm staying as I am.
I'm a human being. A human being. (*He sits in the remain-
ing chair*) It's an impossible situation. It's my fault she's
gone. I meant everything to her. What'll become of her?
That's one more person on my conscience. Poor little thing
left all alone in this world of monsters. Nobody can help me
find her, nobody, because there's nobody left.

(*There are fresh trumpetings and sounds of hectic racings off*) I can't bear the sound of them any longer. (*He rises, moves to the chest of drawers and takes out some cotton wool*) I'm going to put cotton wool in my ears. (*He moves down C, putting the wool in his ears*) The only solution is to convince them—but convince them of what? Can they be changed back? Can they? It would be a labor of Hercules, far beyond me. In any case, to convince them you'd have to talk to them. And to talk to them, I'd have to learn their language. Or they'd have to learn mine. (*He looks in the imaginary mirror*) But what language do I speak? What is my language? Am I talking French? Yes, it must be French. But what is French? I can call it French if I want, and nobody can say it isn't—I'm the only one who speaks it. (*He pauses*) What am I saying? Do I? And what if it's true what Daisy said, and they're the ones in the right? A man's not ugly to look at, not ugly at all. (*He examines himself, passing his hand over his face*) What a funny-looking thing. What do I look like? What? (*He runs to the chest of drawers, takes out a box of photographs, spills them on the floor and kneels beside them*) Photographs! (*He examines the photographs*) Who are all these people? Is it Mr. Papillon—or is it Daisy? And is that Botard or Dudard or Jean? Or is it me? (*He holds up a photograph in each hand*) Now I recognize me; that's me, that's me. That's me, that's me. I'm not good-looking, I'm not good-looking. (*He drops the photographs*) They're the good-looking ones. I was wrong. Oh, how I wish I was like them. (*He rises and moves to the imaginary mirror*) I haven't got any horns, more's the pity. A smooth brow looks so ugly. I need one or two horns to give my sagging face a lift. Perhaps one will grow and I needn't be ashamed any more—then I could go and join them. But it will never grow. (*He looks at the palms of his hands*) My hands are so smooth. Oh, why won't they get rough? (*He undoes his shirt to look at his chest in the mirror*) My skin is so slack. I can't stand this white, hairy body.

(*Trumpetings are heard*) Oh, I'd love to have a hard skin in that wonderful dull green color—a skin that looks decent naked without any hair on it, like theirs. (*He listens to the trumpetings*) Their song is charming—a bit raucous, perhaps, but it does have charm. (*He moves down C*) I wish I could do it. (*He tries to imitate them*) Ahh, Ahh, Brr! No, that's not it. Try again, louder. Ahh, Ahh, Brr! No, that's not it, it's too feeble, it's got no drive behind it. I'm not trumpeting at all; I'm just howling. Ahh, Ahh, Brr! (*He moves up C*) There's a big difference between howling and trumpeting. I've only myself to blame; I should have gone with them while there was still time. Now, it's too late. (*He sees the heads on the back wall and backs from them down C, in horror*) Now I'm a monster, just a monster. Now I'll never become a rhinoceros, never, never. I've gone past changing. (*He puts his hands to his face and turns to the imaginary mirror*) I want to, I really do, but I can't. I just can't. I can't stand the sight of me. I'm too ashamed. (*He moves up C sobbing, and falls on his face, his shoulders heaving*) I'm so ugly. People who try to hang on to their individuality always come to a bad end. (*He pauses, then suddenly snaps out of it, rises, moves down R, grabs the bottle of brandy and a glass and sits on the chair C*) Oh, well, too bad. I'll take on all of them. I'll put up a fight against the lot of them. I'm the last man left, and I'm staying that way until the end. I'm not capitulating.

BERENGER *drinks as a huge cut-out rhinoceros drops in from the flies and the curtain falls.*

ROSS

Terence Rattigan

Aircraftman Ross was the name that Colonel T. E. Lawrence (Lawrence of Arabia) took when he sought anonymity and refuge in the R.A.F. after his exploits in the desert and his self-disillusionment there. Terence Rattigan's play opens in an R.A.F. depot near London in 1922; later, in flashback form, we are shown incidents in Ross's career in the Middle East.

This conversation takes place in a small hut in a British Army camp near Suez. Lawrence has persuaded the famous Sheik Auda Abu Tayi to join him in an attack on the port of Akaba from the land, against odds of four to one. This unexpected attack is successful and Akaba is taken. Now Lawrence is telephoning to Naval Headquarters at Suez to ask for food and ammunition to be sent to Akaba.

It is an interesting speech for the actor because in it are shown Lawrence's dislike of officialdom and red tape, his deliberately casual manner, which infuriated more conventional officers, and his habit of understatement. At this moment he is utterly exhausted physically, hungry and thirsty, but the magnetism of his personality has to be conveyed. Admiral Makepeace's reactions at the other end of the line have to be carefully timed.

ACT I, SCENE viii

LAWRENCE (*into telephone*): Oh, hullo, Admiral. Sorry to disturb you. . . . My name is Lawrence, Captain Lawrence. . . . Oh, no. Just army. Look. I want you to send a destroyer to Akaba . . . destroyer, that's right, but it doesn't have to be a destroyer. As a matter of fact a bigger thing—might be better. It's got to take a lot of stuff, you see—food for five hundred men, about six howitzers, thirty machine guns, as many grenades and rifles as the army will let you have—oh— and some armored cars would come in very handy. Also— most important of all really—about fifty thousand pounds in cash. . . . Fifty thousand. . . . Oh, I'm sorry. Didn't I tell you. . . . Yes, we took it . . . from the land. Rather a long way round, but it seemed to work all right. . . . No. They didn't appear to expect us. . . . Oh, about five hundred killed and seven hundred prisoners. . . . Ours? Two. Unhappily we lost five more on the march, including one of my bodyguard. You see conditions in the desert were a bit—rough. We had three bad sandstorms, and I'm afraid my compass work wasn't all that good, and we missed a well. . . . No, Admiral, I promise you this isn't a joke. Akaba is ours. . . . A rather picturesque fellow called Auda Abu Tayi is holding it, but don't let him sell it to you, because he'll certainly try. Now you will get that boat there tonight, won't you? You see, the Turks are bound to react violently, and mount a counteroffensive in the next few days. Will you please inform Cairo for me? I'm a bit tired. . . . No. I won't be available tomorrow. I shall be asleep tomorrow and probably the next day. If they want to talk to me after that they'll find me in my old office in Cairo. . . . Making maps. . . . Yes. The C.-in-C. does know of me. In fact General Murray and I have often exchanged words. . . . Gone? Gone for good? (*Plainly delighted*) Oh dear! Who, then . . . Allenby? No, I've not heard of him. Thank you, sir. Good night. (*He rings off and rests his head on the desk*)

YES IS FOR A VERY YOUNG MAN

Gertrude Stein

The action of the play begins with the official French capitulation to the Germans during World War II, and ends with the liberation of Paris. We watch the course of the collaboration and the growth of the Resistance against it through the actions of a French family caught in moments of humor, contemplation, despair, and jubilation.

Henry is a serious young man. He has a selfish, comfort-loving wife, whom he loves, two brothers in a German prison, and another idealistic younger one at home. Henry returns from reading the Armistice notice (that of official collaboration), and speaks to his wife and brother, who are shelling peas.

Gertrude Stein's theater pieces have been widely read and studied, less frequently performed. This is no doubt due in large part to her style of language, which is reputedly "difficult." However the structure of her phrasing is often closer to natural speech and/or thought processes than many more regular writings. She uses words as material substance, and it would be unwise of the actor to try to "handle" her words—to bend them to fit a preconceived idea of how the character should sound. Rather, careful attention to the structure of the phrasing will allow the character to grow through the modes of language and rhythm that have been created for him.

ACT I

HENRY: Have you seen the armistice notice?

FERDINAND: No, I couldn't look.

HENRY: I looked, there it was, on the barn, all day yesterday. The rain was coming down, a group of farmers were standing there reading the notice, they didn't say anything, it rained, they read, they went away, and then there it was, it was raining nobody was reading it, nobody, and it was raining and then I saw two of them standing there, and they said, France needs discipline, and then two others stood and read it, and the old one said he couldn't believe it, and I heard his son say, come along old man, of course you can believe it. Well, said the young one, for my generation there is nothing to believe, but your generation, of course you can believe it.

And it just kept on raining and the notice of the armistice

was there on the barn. Oh my God, and it got darker and darker and it rained and it was there, and then I heard Achille, yes your brother Denise, say that there was going to be an army. My God an army, my God, Marshal Petain's army, one hundred and twenty-five thousand men. My God, not a French army, Marshal Petain's army. My God.

Omit Ferdinand's line.

HADRIAN VII
Peter Luke

Peter Luke based his play on *Hadrian VII* and other works by Frederick Rolfe (Baron Corvo). It is a semi-biographical study of this extraordinary man, writer, medievalist, artist and scholar, who died in 1913 after a life of continuous struggle to keep himself by his writings. His books brought him in only small sums and he never received a penny for *Hadrian* (published in 1904) as the publishers stipulated that he should be paid no royalties on the first six hundred copies.

Rolfe was a rejected candidate for the Roman Catholic priesthood but still believed in The Faith. He was always a loner. "I cultivate the gentle art of making enemies," he said. "A friend is necessary, one friend—but an enemy is more necessary. An enemy keeps one alert."

The play describes how the penniless Rolfe receives a visit from two church dignitaries who accept him, belatedly, into the priesthood. Subsequently, on a visit to Rome, as a chaplain at a meeting of the conclave of cardinals to elect a new pope, he is called to the vacant throne and becomes Pope Hadrian VII.

In the opening scene, from which this speech is taken, Rolfe is a slim, agile man of forty. He is nearsighted and wears steel-rimmed spectacles. He smokes heavily, rolling his own cigarettes. His movements are catlike. The landlady of his West Hampsted lodgings has just left him after threatening to turn him out unless he pays his overdue rent.

ROLFE (*shouting in a paroxysm of rage at the closed door*): You can't get manure from a wooden rocking-horse, you rapacious, concupiscent . . . female. (*After a short pause he has second thoughts, runs to the door, opens it and shouts*) Mrs. Crowe! (*There is no answer*)

Mrs. Crowe, I know you're listening. When you're sorry for what you've said, don't be afraid to say so, Mrs. Crowe. (*He closes the door and puts the blanket round his shoulders*) Someone will have to suffer for this. (*He rolls and lights a cigarette, holding it cupped in his two hands for warmth*) All those curves and protuberances— breeding, that's all they're good for. (*He sits*) Jeremiah Sant is a gerrymandering gouger!

(*After a moment he hears footsteps on the stairs again. He listens, wondering if it is Mrs. Crowe coming back to apologize. Instead, a letter is thrust under the door. He rises, looks at it suspiciously, then picks it up and turns it over, looking at the seal*)

What—what's that? Archbishop's house? (*He tears the letter open and reads it with trembling hands. Savagely*) Hell and damnation! Imbeciles! Owl-like hierarchs! Degenerates! (*After a pause*) God, if ever You loved me, hear me. They have denied me the priesthood again. Not a chance do You give me, God—ever. Listen! How can I serve You—(*to the crucifix*)—while you keep me so sequestered? I'm intelligent. So, O God, You made me. But intelligence must be active, potent, and perforce I am impotent and inactive always; futile in my loneliness. Why, O God, have You made me strange, uncommon, such a mystery to my fellow-creatures? Am I such a ruffian as to merit total exile from them? You have made me denuded of the power of love—to love any-

102

body or be loved. I shall always be detached and apart from the others. I suppose I must go on like that to the end (*grimly*) because they are frightened of me—frightened of the labels I put on them. (*He puts out his cigarette savagely*) O God, forgive me smoking. I quite forgot. I am not doing well at present. They force me into it; a pose of haughty genius, subtle, learned, inaccessible. Oh, it's wrong, wrong altogether, but what can I do? God, tell me clearly, unmistakably and distinctly, tell me, tell me what I must do—and make me do it. (*He sits*) O Lord, I am sick—and very tired. (*His mind is in a ferment and he cannot rest*)

(*There is a knock on the door. Fiercely*) Who is it? (*He rises and moves to L of the door*)

A DREAM OF LOVE

William Carlos Williams

Dr. Williams in his autobiography writes of the physician's "lifetime of careful listening." His attention to the essential poetry "hidden under the verbiage" furnishes his characters, unlike those of many poet-playwrights, with all their vital organs. At the same time the flow of his prose has acutely recorded subtle rhythms of American speech.

"Doc" Thurber is a middle-aged general practitioner in a New York suburb. He writes poetry, about which he has misgivings, and loves his wife Myra, although he indulges in occasional affairs. Doc takes the unhappy woman who types his poems to a hotel room with him, and there dies. The rest of the play is concerned with his wife's struggle to resolve her conflicted emotions and to make this last tragedy part of the cohesive structure of their past life together.

The scene takes place in the kitchen where Myra has been

living since Doc last left it. Doc returns, in an insight or dream (the choice is the director's), and the two struggle to reach a level of understanding. She asks him, "What could you tell me that I do not know?"

The actor should avoid playing Doc as a "ghost." His apparent reality makes possible the impact of the scene.

ACT III, SCENE ii

DOC: Well, I'll tell you. A man must protect his pride, his integrity as a man, as best he is able, by whatever invention he can cook up out of his brains or his belly, as the case may be. He must create a woman of some sort out of his imagination to prove himself. Oh, it doesn't have to be a woman, but she's the generic type. It's a woman—even if it's a mathematical formula for relativity. Even more so in that case—but a woman. A woman out of his imagination to match the best. All right, a poem. I mean a woman, bringing her up to the light, building her up and not merely of stone or colors or silly words—unless he's supremely able—but in the flesh, warm, agreeable, made of pure consents. That means they're not married, of course—unless he unmarries them by hard work for a moment now and then. Something—to that time unconceived by him or anyone in the world. Do you follow me?

MYRA: Is that all?

DOC: When a man, of his own powers, small as they are, once possesses his imagination, concretely, grabs it with both hands—he is made! Or lost, I've forgotten which . . . (*He looks at her closely*) And just as a woman must produce out of her female belly to complete herself—a son—so a man must produce a woman, in full beauty out of the shell of his imagination and possess her, to complete himself also . . .

DOC (*speaking now as if to an audience*): This is purely personal—ad interim: He interests his wife in this—she follows his vision—or she does not. She joins him—or she doesn't—in the search for that divine beauty which is not

104

theirs, to be sure, but moves them both, together—or it does not. It is supremely detached from their acts, from all infidelities. It stands in the full light, APART. It is *his* perishable genius, such as it is, which he has hardly won and which she . . . (*He leans over her, studying her intently for a moment*) She is asleep! (*He lights a cigarette and walks about*) I died when I walked upon the grass. I died in everything. I died when I was born. (*He leans over her.*) From which you once rescued me—hence my devotion. (*He sits down on a chair, at some distance from her, and buries his head in his hands*)

Omit Myra's line.

CHARACTER
AND DIALECT

AH, WILDERNESS!

Eugene O'Neill

The play is set in Connecticut in the summer of 1906. Richard, just out of high school, nearly seventeen, is the son of the owner of the local paper.

Eugene O'Neill describes the boy as having a "restless, apprehensive, defiant, shy, dreamy self-conscious intelligence. In manner he is alternately plain simple boy and a posy actor playing a role."

This scene takes place on a strip of beach along the harbor about nine o'clock on the evening after Thanksgiving Day. Richard is waiting for Muriel McComber whose father has forbidden her to leave the house because he thinks that Richard has been trying to corrupt her by encouraging her to read books of a questionable nature. The day before Muriel's father delivered a letter from her to Richard saying that she would have nothing more to do with him. That evening a Yale friend of his brother takes him out with him and he meets a peroxide blonde, a typical college tart of the period, who gets him drunk and tries, unsuccessfully, to seduce him. Eventually the bartender pushes him out of the back room of the bar and he arrives home drunk and disheveled to the consternation of his family. His father forbids him to go out the next day. However, Muriel manages to get a note to him to say that she will try to meet him that evening. He slips out of the house and in this speech is waiting for her to come to the rendezvous. He is torn by conflicting emotions.

ACT IV, SCENE ii

A *strip of beach along the harbor. At left, a bank of dark earth, running half-diagonally back along the beach, marking the line where the sand of the beach ends and fertile land begins. The top of the bank is grassy and the trailing boughs of willow trees extend out over it and over a part of the beach. At left, front, is a path leading up the bank, between the willows. On the beach, at center front, a white, flat-bottomed rowboat is drawn up, its bow about touching the bank, the painter trailing up the bank, evidently made fast to the trunk of a willow. Halfway down the sky, at rear left, the crescent of the new moon casts a soft, mysterious, caressing light over everything. The sand of the beach shimmers palely. The forward half (left of center) of the rowboat is in the deep shadows cast by the willow, the stern section is in moonlight. In the distance, the orchestra of a summer hotel can be heard very faintly at intervals.*

RICHARD *is discovered sitting sideways on the gunwale of the rowboat near the stern. He is facing left, watching the path. He is in a great state of anxious expectancy, squirming about uncomfortably on the narrow gunwale, kicking at the sand restlessly, twirling his straw hat, with a bright-colored band in stripes, around on his finger.*

RICHARD (*thinking aloud*): Must be nearly nine . . . I can hear the Town Hall clock strike, it's so still tonight. . . . Gee, I'll bet Ma had a fit when she found I'd sneaked out. . . . I'll catch hell when I get back, but it'll be worth it . . . if only Muriel turns up . . . she didn't say for certain she could . . . gosh, I wish she'd come! . . . Am I sure she wrote nine? . . . (*He puts the straw hat on the seat amidships and pulls the folded letter out of his pocket and peers at it in the moonlight*) Yes, it's nine, all right. (*He starts to put the note back in his pocket, then stops and kisses it—then shoves it away hastily, sheepish, looking around him shamefacedly as if afraid he were being observed*) Aw, that's

107

silly . . . no, it isn't either . . . not when you're really in love.
. . . (*He jumps to his feet restlessly*) Darn it, I wish she'd
show up! Think of something else . . . that'll make the time
pass quicker. . . . Where was I this time last night? . . .
Waiting outside the Pleasant Beach House . . . Belle . . .
ah, forget her! . . . Now, when Muriel's coming . . . that's
a fine time to think of! . . . But you hugged and kissed her.
. . . Not until I was drunk, I didn't . . . and then it was all
showing off . . . darned fool! . . . And I didn't go upstairs
with her . . . even if she was pretty. . . . Aw, she wasn't pretty
. . . she was all painted up . . . she was just a whore . . . she
was everything dirty. . . . Muriel's a million times prettier
anyway. . . . Muriel and I will go upstairs . . . when we're
married . . . but that will be beautiful . . . but I oughtn't
even to think of that yet . . . it's not right . . . I'd never—
now . . . and she'd never . . . she's a decent girl . . . I couldn't
love her if she wasn't . . . but after we're married. . . . (*He
gives a little shiver of passionate longing—then resolutely
turns his mind away from these improper, almost desecrating
thoughts*) That damned barkeep kicking me. . . . I'll bet
you if I hadn't been drunk I'd have given him one good
punch in the nose, even if he could have licked me after!
. . . (*Then with a shiver of shamefaced revulsion and self-
disgust*) Aw, you deserved a kick in the pants . . . making
such a darned slob of yourself . . . reciting the Ballad of
Reading Gaol to those lowbrows! . . . You must have been
a fine sight when you got home . . . having to be put to
bed and getting sick! . . . Phaw! (*He squirms disgustedly*)
Think of something else, can't you? . . . Recite something.
. . . See if you remember . . .

> "Nay, let us walk from fire unto fire,
> From passionate pain to deadlier delight—
> I am too young to live without desire,
> Too young art thou to waste this summer night—"

Gee, that's a peach! . . . I'll have to memorize the rest and recite it to Muriel the next time. . . . I wish I could write poetry . . . about her and me. . . . (*He sighs and stares around him at the night*) Gee, it's beautiful tonight . . . as if it was a special night . . . for me and Muriel. . . . Gee, I love tonight. . . . I love the sand, and the trees, and the grass, and the water, and the sky, and the moon . . . it's all in me and I'm in it. . . . God, it's so beautiful! (*He stands staring at the moon with a rapt face. From the distance the Town Hall clock begins to strike. This brings him back to earth with a start*) There's nine now. . . . (*He peers at the path apprehensively*) I don't see her . . . she must have got caught . . . (*Almost tearfully*) Gee, I hate to go home and catch hell . . . without having seen her! . . . (*Then calling a manly cynicism to his aid*) Aw, who ever heard of a woman ever being on time. . . . I ought to know enough about life by this time not to expect . . . (*Then with sudden excitement*) There she comes now . . . Gosh! (*He heaves a huge sigh of relief—then recites dramatically to himself, his eyes on the approaching figure*)

And lo my love, mine own soul's heart, more dear
Than mine own soul, more beautiful than God,
Who hath my being between the hands of her—

(*Then hastily*) Mustn't let her know I'm so tickled. . . . I ought to be about that first letter, anyway. . . . If women are too sure of you, they treat you like slaves . . . let her suffer for a change. . . . (*He starts to stroll around with exaggerated carelessness, turning his back on the path, hands in pockets whistling with insouciance "Waiting at the Church." MURIEL McCOMBER enters from down the path, left front. She is fifteen, going on sixteen. She is a pretty girl with a plump, graceful little figure, fluffy, light-brown hair, big naïve wondering dark eyes, a round, dimpled face, a melting drawly voice. Just now she is in a great*

109

thrilled state of timid adventurousness. She hesitates in the shadow at the foot of the path, waiting for RICHARD to see her; but he resolutely goes on whistling with back turned, and she has to call him)
MURIEL: Oh, Dick!
RICHARD (*turns around with an elaborate simulation of being disturbed in the midst of profound meditation*): Oh, hello. Is it nine already? Gosh, time passes—when you're thinking.

Omit Muriel's line.

THE BESPOKE OVERCOAT
Wolf Mankowitz

Wolf Mankowitz describes his play as "a sustained, typically over-long Jewish joke." This speech opens the play. Morry, a Jewish tailor, is talking about his friend Fender, who has asked him to repair a coat that Morry made for him twenty-two years before. Morry tells him that the coat is past repair and offers to make him a new one made to measure. But Fender dies before he gets his bespoke overcoat and Morry suffers from a twinge of the "unreasonable conscience felt by the poor who love the poorer with a love which conquers nothing."

In his lifetime Fender does not get enough food, he does not get his tailor-made overcoat, but he and his friend share a sense of humor and a sense of humility.

SCENE i
MORRY: Fender dead. That old man Fender dead. Funny thing. You're a good tailor, he used to say. You're a good tailor. No, you're a good tailor. Look around. I don't care

110

where you look, he says, you are a number one tailor. Look at this coat, he says. What, that old coat? That coat must be twenty years old. Mind you, I can tell straightaway by the cross-stitch it's my coat. It's your coat, he shouts. You made it. Twenty-two years ago I come to you for a coat. This is him. I still got him. You got a good point. I tell him, I'm a good tailor. It's only the truth. I'm a good tailor. Straightaway, I see I made a mistake. I fell in. How much, Fender says, will you take to mend a coat like this? I ask you, It's falling to pieces on his back. I told him straight, no nonsense. Look, Fender, I told him, I can run you up a pair of trousers from lining canvas you can walk up Saville Road nobody can tell you from the Prince of Wales. But, Fender, do me a favor. Take the coat somewhere else. A new coat I can make, but the Union says no miracles. A rag, that's all. I got my clients to think about. Good afternoon. A lovely piece of worsted. Mind you, I got a suit length here; in a hundred year you wouldn't see nothing better. Clients. Fender dead. An old man. (*Turns US still speaking*) He sits in that stone cold warehouse all day long. (*Turns head round to audience*) Who could mend such a coat? (*Moves slowly US to C exit*) That's enough. (*Light starts to fade*) Leave me alone. All this nagging, nagging. (*He has gone, and so has the light*)

BILLY LIAR
Keith Waterhouse and Willis Hall

Billy Fisher is a kind of North Country Walter Mitty, indulging in daydreams which involve him in highly embarrassing predicaments, such as finding himself engaged to three girls simultaneously. Billy, an imaginative youth of nineteen, is trying desperately to escape from his humdrum lower middle-class industrial background. He is the despair of his stolidly unimaginative family who cannot understand or control him. This speech ends the first act of the play. Billy has been entertaining Barbara, one of his fiancées, and has slipped a "passion pill" into her drink. Now, while she is out of the room, he takes the opportunity of adding more, in fact the entire contents of the bottle. Mr. Duxbury, one of the partners in the undertaking firm for whom Billy works, telephones to find out why he has not come to work that morning. These two telephone conversations, one real, one imaginary, show Billy at his most inventive.

ACT I

The telephone rings in the hall. He places the glass on the table and crosses into the hall where he picks up the phone. BILLY: The Fisher residence. Can I help you? (*His manner changes*) Oh, hullo, Mr. Duxbury. No, well, I'm sorry but I've had an accident. I was just leaving for work and I spilled this hot water down my arm. I had to get it bandaged. . . . Oh, well, I think there's a very simple explanation for that, Mr. Duxbury. You see, there's a lot of those figures that haven't been carried forward. . . . I use my own individual system. . . . No. No, not me, Mr. Duxbury. Well, I'm sure you'll find that there's a very simple explanation. . . . What? Monday morning? Yes, of course I'll be there. Prompt. Thank you, Mr. Duxbury. Thank you for ringing. Good-bye, then. . . . (*BILLY puts down the telephone for a moment and is lost in depression. He brightens as, in his imagination, he addresses his employer*) Well, look Duxbury —we're not going to argue over trivialities. As soon as I've finalized my arrangements with Mr. Boon I'll get in touch with you. (*He picks up the telephone*) Hello, Duxbury? . . . I'm afraid the answer is "no." I fully agree that partnership sounds very attractive—but frankly my interests lie in other directions. I'm quite willing to invest in your business, but I just have not the time to take over the administrative

112

side. . . . Oh, I agree that you have a sound proposition there. . . . Granted! I take your point, Mr. Duxbury. What's that little saying of yours? "You've got to come down to earth." It's not a question of coming down to earth, old man. Some of us belong in the stars. The best of luck, Mr. Duxbury, and keep writing. . . . (*BILLY breaks off as BAR-BARA approaches down the stairs and, for her benefit, he goes into another fantasy as she passes him and enters the living room.*) Well, doctor, if the leg's got to come off—it's got to come off. . . . (*BILLY replaces the telephone and looks speculatively at the living room door*) It's not a question of coming down to earth, Mr. Duxbury. (*He pauses*) Some of us, Mr. Duxbury, belong in the stars.

THE BROWNING VERSION
Terence Rattigan

Andrew Crocker-Harris has been form master of the lower fifth in a public school in the south of England for eighteen years. Now he is having to retire prematurely owing to a heart condition. Millie, his wife, has been having an affair with Frank Hunter, a younger member of the staff, and has not troubled to conceal the fact from Andrew. In this scene, Hunter has just witnessed evidence of Millie's cruelty to her husband. Taplow, one of the boys, has presented him with a copy of Browning's translation of *The Agamemnon*. Andrew, who realizes that he has never been popular with the boys, is greatly moved by the gift. When Millie is told of it she remarks that Taplow is an artful little beast and goes on to say, "I came into this room this afternoon to find him giving an imitation of you to Frank here. Obviously he was scared stiff I was going to tell you, and you'd ditch his remove or something. I don't blame him for

113

trying a few bob's worth of appeasement." Hunter is so shocked and disgusted by this incident that he later tells Millie that their affair, which was of her seeking anyway, is finished. When he hears from Andrew that Millie herself told him about the two occasions when she deceived him, he urges Andrew to leave her because she is evil. Andrew refuses to do this, because he says that he does not wish to add to the wrong that he has already done her by marrying her. He explains what he means in this speech. Andrew is described by Terence Rattigan as being neat and unruffled in appearance. He speaks in a very gentle voice.

ANDREW: You see, my dear Hunter, she is really quite as much to be pitied as I. We are both of us interesting subjects for your microscope (*He sits on the fender*) Both of us needing from the other something that would make life supportable for us, and neither of us able to give it. Two kinds of love. Hers and mine. Worlds apart, as I know now, though when I married her I didn't think they were incompatible. In those days I hadn't thought that her kind of love—the love she requires and which I was unable to give her—was so important that its absence would drive out the other kind of love—the kind of love that I require and which I thought, in my folly, was by far the greater part of love. (*He rises*) I may have been, you see, Hunter, a brilliant classical scholar, but I was woefully ignorant of the facts of life. I know better now, of course. I know that in both of us, the love that we should have borne each other has turned to bitter hatred. That's all the problem is. Not a very unusual one, I venture to think—nor nearly as tragic as you seem to imagine. Merely the problem of an unsatisfied wife and a henpecked husband. You'll find it all over the world. It is usually, I believe, a subject for farce. (*He turns to the mantelpiece and adjusts the hands of the clock*) And now, if you have to leave us, my dear fellow, please don't let me detain you any longer.

A CRADLE OF WILLOW

Dorothy Wright

This nativity play is set in a master basket maker's shed in fen country. However, the author, Dorothy Wright, says of it, "This play has no time and no setting but the time and place everyone gives it—the morning of his world and the fens of his own country." The time, she says, is that of the old days of master craftsmen before the use of gunpowder.

It may be played in any country dialect, though the sound in the author's ears was that of the West Country.

Martin has been a wild-fowler in his youth. Now in his late thirties he is blind and although he is able to keep himself by basket-making, he is bitter about his affliction. He has never forgotten the sight of the geese in flight. Here he is talking to Will, a young apprentice. Will has asked him, "Did you go blind all at once?" This speech is his answer.

ACT I

MARTIN: No, it was months coming. Gradual—like the mist coming up over the sedges. Clear first, then blurred a little, at the edges of the world. Early one morning I could hear the skeins of geese go honkin' over, but when I looked up I couldn't see 'em. I rubbed my eyes and still I couldn't and yet the sky was bright and I knew it was full of 'em. You know the way they come, like armies in triumph. I sat down on the edge of the dyke and then I knew the full of it; all I wouldn't believe had been coming all that time. The span'l knew too; he came and put his muzzle into my hand. So I got up at last and I went to Master Breague where he was cutting withes and I said to 'im, "Master, I'm goin' blind. I'm no more good to you as a fowler; you'd better find another man. I can train up the old dog to beg for me." Oh they was good to me, boy. I'll never say other than that. Master took me to the apothecary and Mistress brewed wild herbs to put on my eyes; but it was no good. Day by

115

day, and bit by bit, the sight went out of my eyes. It was then that Master had the idea I should work in here. First it was only stripping and stacking but soon I couldn't even see enough for that. One day Hoad sat me down at the plank, to keep me out of mischief he said, and he got me plaiting rushes. That's how it started, but that's how it's gone on these ten long years. Now I'm a blind basket maker who can hold his own with any worker of willow throughout the land—coarse willow, not the fine fancies.

Master Martin! Master basket maker. Do you think I wouldn't exchange every bit of my skill for one sight of the sedge and the geese going over? Or the sight of her. . . . No. . . . (*He breaks into his shrill wild whistling. Suddenly he stands up and half turns toward the door UL as he puts two fingers to his mouth and lets out a call that goes through your head. MARTIN laughs*) That's set the falcons dancing on their perches and the span'ls straining at the leash. Here sits Martin the hunter, blind as a post. Martin's calling. Who will come and hunt with Martin in the dark?

THE ENTERTAINER

John Osborne

Archie, a broken-down, corny, music hall comedian, is playing in an unsuccessful holiday show *Rock 'n' Roll New'd Look* in a seaside town. Phoebe, his second wife, and Billy his father—a performer from the heyday of the musical hall—live with him. Jean, his daughter by his first marriage, comes to see them and he is speaking to her here. He is drunk and Osborne says "he sings and orchestrates his speech as only a drunken man can."

Archie realizes that his emotions are dead; he can no longer feel anything. Neither can the people round him, the people that he meets every day and also his audiences. The capacity to feel has died in the same way as the music hall with its songs and its enthusiasms is dying. Later in the scene he says "I'm dead behind these eyes. I'm dead, just like the whole inert, shoddy lot out there. It doesn't matter because I don't feel a thing, and neither do they. We're just as dead as each other." But first he describes to Jean an incident in his past life when he heard an old black woman singing in a bar, "singing her heart out to the whole world," and her emotion succeeded in stirring something in him. "I've never heard anything like that since," Archie says, "I've never heard it here."

NO. 8

ARCHIE *is drunk, and he sings and orchestrates his speech as only a drunken man can, almost objectively and fastidiously, like a conductor controlling his own sound.*

ARCHIE: Yes, I loved her. I was in love with her, whatever that may mean. I don't know. Anyway, a few months later she was dead and that was that. She felt everything very deeply, your mother. Much more deeply than I did. Perhaps we could have worked it out between us. She'd never been poor and lonely, or oppressed, but somehow, in some strange peculiar way of her own, she could feel things that were done to her. Do you know the most moving thing that I ever heard? It was when I was in Canada—I managed to slip over the border sometimes to some people I knew, and one night I heard some Negress singing in a bar. *Now you're going to smile at this,* you're going to smile your educated English head off, because I suppose you've never sat lonely and half slewed in some bar among strangers a thousand miles from anything you think you understand. But if ever I saw any hope or strength in the human race, it was in the face of that old fat Negress getting up to sing about Jesus or something like that. She was poor and lonely and oppressed like nobody you've ever known. Or me, for that matter. I never even liked that kind of music, but to see that old black whore singing

117

her heart out to the whole world, you knew somehow in your heart that it didn't matter how much you kick people, the real people, how much you despise them, if they can stand up and make a pure, just natural noise like that, there's nothing wrong with them, only with everybody else. I've never heard anything like that since. I've never heard it here. Oh, I've heard whispers of it on a Saturday night somewhere. Oh, he's heard it. Billy's heard it. He's heard them singing. Years ago, poor old gubbins. But you won't hear it anywhere now. I don't suppose we'll ever hear it again. There's nobody who can feel like that. I wish to God I could, I wish to God I could feel like that old black bitch with her fat cheeks, and sing. If I'd done one thing as good as that in my whole life, I'd have been all right. Better than all your getting on with the job without making a fuss, or doing something constructive and all that, all your rallies in Trafalgar Square! I wish to God I were that old bag. I'd stand up and shake my great bosom up and down and lift up my head and make the most beautiful fuss in the world. Dear God, I would. But I'll never do it. I don't give a damn about anything, not even women or draught Bass. Do you think that you're going to do it? Well, do you?

THE HAMLET OF STEPNEY GREEN

Bernard Kops

Bernard Kops's play was written in 1956. It is set in the East End of London, in Stepney Green. Sam is a pickled-herring seller of sixty-five. The speech is taken from the first act, during which he is dying—but he has so often recovered before that

118

no one pays much attention to him now. He is a frail old man and has ordered his bed to be pushed into the garden. He has got out of his bed in his pyjamas and is walking round the stage and puffing at a cigar and looking at imaginary fruit and groceries, remembering his past life while he talks to Mr. Segal, a friend of the family. At the end of the act Sam dies. The writing is very free and the characters in the play sometimes sing, sometimes address the audience directly. Bernard Kops uses Sam as a mouthpiece through which he tilts at the hypocrisy of our times.

ACT I

SAM: After all, that is all that there is in life, going places and seeing people, different places, different people. I promised myself a world trip before I died, to see for myself how people in other countries lived. It never transpired. Working in the market makes you curious; it does that for you. . . . You see the colored labels stuck upon the boxes, and you think of the man who packed those boxes, and of the girl who stuck that label on. You think of the sun beating down on the wharves and the boat being loaded by sweating men, gently swaying in the golden waves; but—it's too late for the holiday you planned and you never left the market where you stand. Beggars can't be choosers, Mr. Segal, and my only regret is not traveling, not having seen California and the Caucasus, Haifa and Helsinki; I never even saw Odessa again, not that I ever saw it really. I came on an onion boat to Tilbury when I was fourteen. Boxes and boxes of onions on that boat, all with labels stuck on saying "Onions, made in Russia." I was also made in Russia, so I came to Tilbury, and then I came here and I have been here ever since.

I'M TALKING ABOUT JERUSALEM
Arnold Wesker

This play, which appeared in 1960, is the third in Wesker's trilogy and follows *Roots*. It completes the story of the Kahns, the Jewish East End family.

In Act I Ada Kahn and her husband Dave have arrived at their cottage in Norfolk where they hope to live a life dedicated to craftsmanship. They have a dream of existence inspired by William Morris. In the second act Dave is disillusioned; he discovers that the making of furniture on the lines that he has planned is not economically sound. At the end of the play Dave and Ada decide to return to London. Their experiment has been a failure. In this speech, spoken to Ronnie, his brother-in-law, just before they leave the cottage, Dave expresses his disillusion and recognizes that "as an essential member of society I don't really count."

ACT III, SCENE ii

DAVE: What do you think I am, Ronnie? You think I'm an artist's craftsman? Nothing of that sort. A designer? Not even that. Designers are ten-a-penny. I don't mind, Ronnie— Believe me I don't. (*But he does*) I've reached the point where I can face the fact that I'm not a prophet. Once I had—I don't know—a, a moment of vision, and I yelled at your Aunty Esther that I was a prophet. A prophet! Poor woman, I don't think she understood. All I meant was I was a sort of spokesman. That's all. But it passed. Look, I'm a bright boy. There aren't many flies on me and when I was younger I was even brighter. I was interested and alive to everything, history, anthropology, philosophy, architecture— I had ideas. But not now. Not now, Ronnie. I don't know— it's sort of sad this what I'm saying, it's a sad time for both of us—Ada and me—sad, yet—you know—it's not all that sad. We came here, we worked hard, we've loved every minute of it and we're still young. Did you expect anything else? You wanted us to grow to be giants, didn't you? The mighty artist craftsman! Well, now the only things that seem to matter to me are the day-to-day problems of my wife, my kids and my work. Face it—as an essential member of society I don't really count. I'm not saying that I'm useless but machinery and modern techniques have come about to make me the odd man out. Here I've been, comrade citizen, presenting my offerings and the world's rejected them. I don't count, Ronnie, and if I'm not sad about it you mustn't be either. Maybe Sarah's right, maybe you can't build on your own.

THE LONG AND THE SHORT AND THE TALL

Willis Hall

The time is 1942, before the fall of Singapore and the Japanese offensive down the Malayan mainland. A patrol of British soldiers is on active service in the Malayan jungle. Sergeant Mitchem, a seasoned soldier, is in charge of an inexperienced group of men. Earlier in the play they have taken a Japanese prisoner and are sheltering in a hut, preparing to make their way back, through the jungle and the enemy surrounding them, to their unit. Mitchem does not relish the task of having to kill their Japanese prisoner before they go. The lance-corporal's sympathetic attitude to the prisoner irritates him because he is afraid that he himself will weaken toward the prisoner. Here it is perhaps suggested that Mitchem has had bitter experience of personal relationships with women. His apparent strength conceals weakness and uncertainty.

ACT II

MITCHEM: It's right. Straight up. They cause more upset than enough. Half the scrapping in this world is over judies. There's half the blokes out here now who'd be sitting back in Blightly still with wangled home postings if it wasn't for a bint. It's bints who go a bundle over uniforms. You take a bloke—an ordinary bloke who gets called up. He doesn't want to go. He doesn't want to come out here, or if he does he's round the bend. Then, one day, this poor Charlie winds up with a bird—it happens to us all in the end. A blonde bird, happen, with small brains and big breasts. She whips him up the dancers once and that's the end of that. She likes the color of his uniform and that makes him feel big. Six months before he was sitting behind a desk, copping on a weekly, picking his nose and chatting up the pigeons on the window sill. Now—all at once—he feels like he's a man. Before he knows where he is he's standing on the boat deck and the bint's waving him off from the docks with a bitsy hanky and tears clogging up her powder. My hero stuff. The captain blows the whistle on the bridge. The gangplank's up. There's a military band on the quay-side, best boots and battledress, playing "Where was the Engine Driver?" "Good-bye Dolly, I must leave you." So there stands Charlie Harry, five foot four in his socks, and feeling like he's Clive of India, Alexander the Great and Henry Five rolled into one.

THE LONG AND THE SHORT AND THE TALL

Willis Hall

Private Whitaker is not a particularly attractive character. He is unpopular with the other men, who call him Fanny because there is something priggish about him. But in this speech to Smith about his girl back home, his youth and uncertainty have an appeal.

ACT II

WHITAKER: She's . . . well, she's sort of pretty, you know, like. Mary. That's her name. Mary Pearson. Comes up to about my shoulder and sort of yellowish hair. Works for an insurance company. In the office. Oh, she's . . . she's bloody pretty, Smudge. Nothing outstanding, like—but, boy, she's pretty. We was courting for three months very nearly. I was up there doing my basic training.

I used to get to meet her a couple of times a week, like. Whenever I could skive off. Get the bus from camp center into Darlington and meet her nights outside a shop. Some nights we'd go to the pictures—or dancing—or something—when I could afford it, like. I wasn't loaded them days. So most nights we'd just walk up through the park, you know. Along by the river. The middle of summer I was at Catterick. Was it hot then, boy! Oh, man! . . . She's only seventeen just—is it a bit young, do you think?

So we'd just walk along by the side of the river, like. Up as far as the bridge. Happen sit down and watch them playing bowls. Sit for ten minutes or so, get up and walk back. Just a steady stroll, you know. I never had much money—only my bus fare there and back sometimes—but it was . . . oh, boy! Oh, you know—we had some smashing times together me and her. I wish I was back there now, boy.

123

THE MULBERRY BUSH

Angus Wilson

Kurt Landeck is twenty-three or twenty-four, a young half-Jewish refugee from the Hitler régime. His father was gassed by the Nazis, his mother afterwards married a Nazi. Kurt is a protégé of Mr. Padley, warden of a university college, who is about to retire and of his wife, Rose, an earnest social worker who is more interested in causes than in human beings. She has never thought of Kurt as having grown up from the small homeless boy that she took in, into an individual with a mind of his own. He was, as he tells her, "only a bit of decoration on the Padley cake. Well," he goes on, "that cake is now crumbling, so the decoration, too, falls off." Kurt has become a parasite in the Padley household, bitterly resentful of patronage.

Angus Wilson describes him as "the new spirit of a violent Europe which is fighting to destroy the humane world the Padleys take for granted." In this telephone conversation he is talking to Lady Heppell, wife of the new warden who has asked him to live with them when they take over the warden's house, and to continue with his writing. In his speech to Rose afterwards he shows the depth of his malice and violence.

ACT III

KURT: What a wonderful smell of decay about the house this morning! It's always so, you know, after storms. . . . (*He goes to the telephone*) Three-nine-four-three-two, please. Hello. Can I speak to Lady Heppell? (*Pause*) Oh, good morning! Lady Heppell? This is Kurt Landeck speaking. (*As he is talking, ROSE comes into the room through french windows and sits at desk*) I have been thinking of your kind offer, Lady Heppell. It is not always that people appreciate the needs of the younger generation as you do. No, that I mean really. But of course you are doing it because you believe in me as a writer. I should not wish you to think of anything else. It is this I accept. Well, then, that is settled.

124

No, I have some visits to pay and I shall not be very good with movings. So September I shall come back to you here. Good-bye. And please to remember you have made me a very happy young man. (*He puts down the telephone and waits for ROSE to speak, but she sits at her desk and begins to write letters.*)

(*With sudden excess of malice at her disregarding him*) I'm sure you must be so glad to know that one of us will be staying on in the old home, Mrs. Padley. (*As she still does not look up*) One of your own disciples to keep the torch of humanity burning amid the brazen waste of Lady Heppell's tasteless rule. (*He waits for her to speak*) Perhaps you think I have not learned my lesson well enough! Listen! (*Crosses D kneels with arms on stool*) I will recite —tolerance, pity, courage, learning—how does it go on?— patronage, interference, pushing people around, patting oneself on the back.

THE PLAYBOY OF THE WESTERN WORLD

J. M. Synge

"Among the best bitter-sweet comedies in the language" is how this play has been described. J. M. Synge based his imaginative prose style on the dialect of the Irish countryfolk—that of the fishermen and herdsmen along the coast from Kerry to Mayo. He said that in a good play "every speech should be as fully flavored as a nut or apple." Christy Mahon, a tired, slight, shy young man, has arrived at a country pub on a wild coast of Mayo the day before. He has announced to the publican and his daughter, Pegeen Mike, and to their friends that he killed

125

his father the day before by striking him on the head with a heavy piece of wood. Later, as he and Pegeen Mike are getting to know one another, they are interrupted by the formidable Widow Quinn. She has heard of Christy's arrival and has come to invite him to lodge with her. Pegeen, furious, says that Christy is going to be employed as pot-boy to the inn and refuses to let him go. After some argument between the two women, the Widow Quinn retires defeated.

As Christy is arranging his bed for the night he reflects "Well, it's a clean bed and soft with it, and it's great luck and company I've won me in the end of time—two fine women fighting for the likes of me—till I'm thinking this night wasn't I a foolish fellow not to kill my father in the years gone by," and the curtain falls on Act One.

Act Two begins with the speech given here. It is next morning, a shiny day. Christy, looking bright and cheerful, is cleaning a girl's boots.

ACT II

CHRISTY (to himself, counting jugs on dresser): Half a hundred beyond. Ten there. A score that's above. Eighty jugs. Six cups and a broken one. Two plates. A power of glasses. Bottles, a school master'd be hard set to count, and enough in them, I'm thinking, to drunken all the wealth and wisdom of the County Clare. (He puts down the boot carefully) There's her boots now, nice and decent for her evening use, and isn't it grand brushes she has? (He puts them down and goes by degrees to the looking glass) Well, this'd be a fine place to be my whole life talking out with swearing Christians, in place of my old dogs and cat; and I stalking around, smoking my pipe and drinking my fill, and never a day's work but drawing a cork an odd time, or wiping a glass, or rinsing out a shiny tumbler for a decent man. (He takes the looking glass from the wall and puts it on the back of a chair, then sits down in front of it and begins washing his face) Didn't I know rightly I was handsome, though it was the divil's own mirror we had beyond, would

126

twist a squint across an angel's brow; and I'll be growing fine from this day, the way I'll have a soft lovely skin on me and won't be the like of the clumsy young fellows do be ploughing all times in the earth and dung. (*He starts*) Is she coming again? (*He looks out*) Stranger girls. God help me, where'll I hide myself away and my long neck naked to the world? (*He looks out*) I'd best go to the room maybe till I'm dressed again. (*He gathers up his coat and the looking glass, and runs into the inner room*)

THE POTTING SHED
Graham Greene

The scene is the sitting room in Father Callifer's presbytery in an East Anglian town. Graham Greene describes the priest as having a "stubbly worn face with bloodshot eyes; a dirty wisp of a Roman collar has been made by twisting and folding a handkerchief round the top of his shirt." Father Callifer has already been turned out of two parishes for drinking and neglecting his flock. This evening his nephew James has come to see him. His housekeeper, Miss Connolly, unaware of who the visitor is, has asked him to wait. He is now in the hall outside. When Father Callifer appears, Miss Connolly tells him that she has discovered his new hiding place for his whisky that morning. She upbraids him for his way of life and asks him not to turn away the man who is waiting outside to see him.

"Father," she asks him, "what kind of a priest are you?" In the following bitter and disillusioned lines he tells her.

ACT II, SCENE ii
MISS CONNOLLY: Father, what kind of a priest are you?
CALLIFER: A priest who does his job. I say the Mass, I

127

hear Confessions, if anyone has a stomach-ache in the night, don't I go to him. Who has ever asked for me and I haven't come?

MISS CONNOLLY: Miss Alexander.

CALLIFER (*slowly with shame*): Yes, you would remind me of that.

MISS CONNOLLY: I couldn't wake you. I had to say next day you were sick. Sick!

CALLIFER: Miss Connolly, you've looked after a lot of priests. You take it as your right to speak your mind to them. And me—you expect me to serve you, all of you, every day for twenty-four hours. I mustn't be a man. I must be a priest. And in return after Mass you give me coffee and eggs (in all these years you've never learned how to make coffee) and you make my bed. You keep my two rooms clean—or nearly. (*He runs his finger along the mantelpiece*) I don't ask you for any more than you are paid to do.

MISS CONNOLLY: These people here have a right to a priest with the faith.

CALLIFER: Faith! They want a play-actor. They want snow-white hair, high collars, clean vestments (who pays the cleaner?—not their sixpences), and they want a voice that's never husky with the boredom of saying the same words day after day. All right. Let them write to the bishop. Do you think I want to get up every morning at six in time to make my meditation before Mass? Meditation on what? The reason why I'm going on with this slave labor? They give prisoners useless tasks, don't they, digging pits and filling them up again. Like mine.

MISS CONNOLLY: Speak low. You don't understand what you are saying, Father.

CALLIFER: Father! I hate the word. I had a brother who believed in nothing, and for thirty years now I have believed in nothing too. A father belongs to his children until they grow up and he's free of them. But these people will never

128

grow up. They die children and leave children behind them. I'm condemned to being a father for life.

Omit all Miss Connolly's lines.

PYGMALION

G. B. Shaw

Pygmalion was published in 1912. It has been turned into the famous musical version *My Fair Lady* and also filmed. The characters of Professor Higgins, Eliza and her father, Alfred Doolittle, have become almost too well known to need describing, but this is the lead-up to Doolittle's speech. Professor Higgins, a professor of phonetics and author of *Higgins' Universal Alphabet*, and Colonel Pickering, author of *Spoken Sanscrit*, have met by chance the previous evening in Covent Garden market where Higgins has been taking notes on the speech of a flower-girl, Eliza.

The next morning Higgins has been demonstrating his collection of vowel sounds to Pickering in Higgins' laboratory in Wimpole Street, when Eliza calls to see him, demanding to be given lessons in phonetics for which she offers to pay a shilling an hour.

Pickering bets the professor that he can't pass Eliza off as a duchess at an ambassador's garden party in three months' time. Higgins takes him on and Eliza is despatched with Mrs. Pearce, ths housekeeper, to be thoroughly scrubbed in the bathroom.

At this moment Alfred Doolittle, Eliza's father, "an elderly but vigorous dustman, clad in the costume of his profession, including a hat with a back brim covering his head and shoulders," appears. "He has well-marked and rather interesting features and seems equally free from fear and conscience. He has a remarkably expressive voice, the result of a habit of giving vent to his feelings without reserve. His present pose is that of wounded honor and stern resolution."

Doolittle has ostensibly come to collect his daughter, but it transpires that he is willing for her to remain in the Higgins ménage on payment to him of the sum of five pounds as he says that he knows that Higgins's intentions are honorable. If he had thought they weren't, he says, he would have asked for fifty pounds. When Pickering explodes, "Have you no morals, man?" Doolittle replies, unabashed, "Can't afford them, governor. Neither could you if you was as poor as me." This speech follows.

ACT II

DOOLITTLE: Don't say that, governor. Don't look at it that way. What am I, governors both? I ask you, what am I? I'm one of the undeserving poor, that's what I am. Think of what that means to a man. It means that he's up agen middle-class morality all the time. If there's anything going, and I put in for a bit of it, it's always the same story: "You're undeserving; so you can't have it." But my needs is as great as the most deserving widows that ever got money out of six different charities in one week for the death of the same husband. I don't need less than a deserving man; I need more. I don't eat less hearty than him, and I drink a lot more. I want a bit of amusement, 'cause I'm a thinking man. I want cheerfulness and a song and a band when I feel low. Well, they charge me just the same for everything as they charge the deserving. What is middle-class morality? Just an excuse for never giving me anything. Therefore, I ask you, as two gentlemen, not to play that game on me. I'm playing straight with you. I ain't pretending to be deserving. I'm undeserving; and I mean to go on being undeserving. I like it, and that's the truth. Will you take advantage of a man's nature to do him out of the price of his own daughter what he's brought up and fed and clothed by the sweat of his brow until she's growed big enough to be interesting to you two gentlemen? Is five pounds unreasonable? I put it to you; and I leave it to you.

UNDER MILK WOOD

Dylan Thomas

Under Milk Wood was first broadcast in 1954, and has subsequently been produced on the stage. It tells the story of a
day in the life of a small Welsh seaside town, Llaregyb. We see
a cross section of its inhabitants engaged in their everyday
affairs. Dylan Thomas uses two narrators, First and Second
Voice, to link the various episodes. They are detached from the
main action and could perhaps best be described as sympathetic
observers. The First Voice introduces and closes the play. This
speech is the opening one. It is spoken on a half-lit stage. In
the preface to this edition Daniel Jones, the poet's friend, has
a note on the pronunciation. "In case *Under Milk Wood* falls
into the hands of a Welsh philologist, it must be made clear
that the language used is Anglo-Welsh. Dylan Thomas spoke no
Welsh, and the reader must imitate his inconsistency if he wishes
to hear the words as they were pronounced by the poet himself.
A note on pronunciation will be found at the end of the text."

In the original stage version, First Voice was standing on a
rostrum for the first part of the speech.

(Silence)

FIRST VOICE (*Very softly*): To begin at the beginning:
It is spring, moonless night in the small town, starless and
bible-black, the cobbled streets silent and the hunched,
courters'—and—rabbits' wood limping invisible down to the
sloeblack, slow, black, crowblack, fishingboat-bobbing sea.
The houses are blind as moles (though moles see fine tonight
in the snouting velvet dingles) or blind as Captain Cat there
in the muffled middle by the pump and the town clock, the
shops in mourning, the Welfare Hall in widows' weeds. And
all the people of the lulled and dumbfound town are sleeping now.

Hush, the babies are sleeping, the farmers, the fishers,
the tradesmen and pensioners, cobblers, schoolteacher, post-

131

man and publican, the undertaker and the fancy woman, drunkard, dress-maker, preacher, policeman, the webfoot cocklewoman and the tidy wives. Young girls lie bedded soft or glide in their dreams, with rings and trousseaux, bridesmaided by glow-worms down the aisles of the organ-playing wood. The boys are dreaming wicked or of the bucking branches of the night and the jollyrodgered sea. And the anthracite statues of the horses sleep in the fields, and the cows in the byres, and the dogs in the wetnosed yards; and the cats nap in the slant corners or lope sly, streaking and needling, on the one cloud of the roofs.

You can hear the dew falling, and the hushed town breathing. Only *your* eyes are unclosed to see the black and folded town fast, and slow, asleep. And you alone can hear the invisible starfall, the darkest-before-dawn minutely dew-grazed stir of the black, dab-filled sea where the *Arethusa*, the *Curlew* and the *Skylark*, *Zanzibar*, *Rhiannon*, the *Rover*, the *Cormorant*, and the *Star of Wales* tilt and ride.

Listen. It is night moving in the streets, the processional salt slow musical wind in Coronation Street and Cockle Row, it is the grass growing on Llaregyb Hill, dewfall, star-fall, the sleep of birds in Milk Wood.

OH DAD, POOR DAD, MAMMA'S HUNG YOU IN THE CLOSET AND I'M FEELIN' SO SAD

Arthur Kopit

The scene is a lavish hotel suite somewhere in the Caribbean. Madame Rosepettle arrives followed by minions bearing the things with which she travels: her husband's coffin (complete with husband), two snapping Venus's-flytraps, a Piranha fish named Rosalinda, treasure chests filled with stamp and coin collections, a dictaphone into which she dictates her memoirs, specially designed accouterments of all sorts, and her son, whose name she won't remember. His name is Jonathan. He feeds the Venus's-flytraps and watches for airplanes and life from the balcony of the hotel. Life comes to him in the shape of Rosalie. She is two years older than he is, and he is not as young as he is treated. She asks him why he can't go out. The speech is his answer.

SCENE 2

JONATHAN: I—I don't know. I don't know why. I mean. I've—nnnnnnnnnnever really thought—about going out. I—guess it's—just natural for me to—stay inside. (*He laughs nervously as if that explained everything*) You see—I've got so much to do. I mean, all my sssssstamps and—ca-coins and books. The pa-pa-plane might fffffffly overhead while I was going downstairs. And then thhhhere are—the plants ta-to feeeeeeed. And I enjoy vvvery much wa—watching you and all yyyyyyour chil-dren. I've—really got so ma-many things—to do. Like—like my future, for instance. Ma-Mother says I'm going to be great. That's—that's—that's what she—says. I'm going to be great. I sssswear. Of course, she doesn't know ex-actly what I'm—going to be great in—so she sits every afternoon for—for two hours and thinks about it. Na-na-naturally I've—got to be here when she's thinking in case

133

she—thinks of the answer. Otherwise she might forget and I'd never know—what I'm ga-going to be great in. You—see what I mean? I mean, I've—I've ggggggot so many things to do I—just couldn't possibly get *anything* done if I ever—went—outside. (*There is a silence.* JONATHAN *stares at* ROSALIE *as if he were hoping that might answer her question sufficiently. She stares back at him as if she knows there is more*) Besides, Mother locks the front door.

THE AMERICAN DREAM
Edward Albee

The Young Man arrives at Mommy and Daddy's apartment looking for work and remains to "give satisfaction." He describes himself as being "almost insultingly good-looking in a typically American way," and says he will do anything for money, for he has no talents at all—except his person. He has no illusions and no hope. In another of Albee's one-act plays, *The Sandbox*, the same character assumes the aspect of the Angel of Death.

He tells this story to Grandma because she is very old, and because she admits knowledge of ridicule and neglect. He tells it without self-pity, and if the actor avoids sentimentality the character can become terrifying in his empty charm. He is the American Dream of the title.

The play has been described as a comic nightmare, but it is also a morality play, a condemnation of the substitution of false values for real ones.

YOUNG MAN: Then listen. My mother died the night that I was born, and I never knew my father; I doubt my mother did. But, I wasn't alone, because lying with me . . . in the placenta . . . there was someone else . . . my brother . . . my twin.

134

GRANDMA: Oh, my child.

YOUNG MAN: We were identical twins . . . he and I . . . not fraternal . . . identical; we were derived from the same ovum; and in *this*, in that we were twins not from separate ova but from the same one, we had a kinship such as you cannot imagine. We . . . we felt each other breathe . . . his heartbeats thundered in my temples . . . mine in his . . . our stomachs ached and we cried for feeding at the same time . . . are you old enough to understand?

GRANDMA: I think so, child; I think I'm nearly old enough.

YOUNG MAN: I hope so. But we were separated when we were still very young, my brother, my twin and I . . . inasmuch as you can separate one being. We were torn apart . . . thrown to opposite ends of the continent. I don't know what became of my brother . . . to the rest of myself . . . except that, from time to time, in the years that have passed, I have suffered losses . . . that I can't explain. A fall from grace . . . a departure of innocence . . . loss . . . loss. How can I put it to you? All right; like this: Once . . . it was as if all at once my heart . . . became numb . . . almost as though I . . . almost as though . . . just like that . . . it had been wrenched from my body . . . and from that time I have been unable to love. Once . . . I was asleep at the time . . . I awoke, and my eyes were burning. And since that time I have been unable to see anything, *anything*, with pity, with affection . . . with anything but . . . cool disinterest. And my groin . . . even there . . . since one time . . . one specific agony . . . since then I have not been able to *love* anyone with my body. And even my hands . . . I cannot touch another person and feel love. And there is more . . . there are more losses, but it all comes down to this: I no longer have the capacity to feel anything. I have no emotions. I have been drained, torn asunder . . . disemboweled. I have, now, only my person . . . my body, my

135

face. I use what I have . . . I let people love me . . . I accept
the syntax around me, for while I know I cannot relate . . .
I know I must be related *to*. I let people love me . . . I let
people touch me . . . I let them draw pleasure from my
groin . . . from my presence . . . from the fact of me . . .
but, that is all it comes to. As told you, I am incomplete
. . . I can feel nothing. I can feel nothing. And so . . . here
I am . . . as you see me. I am . . . but this . . . what you
see. And it will always be thus.

Omit Grandma's lines.

KEEP TIGHTLY CLOSED IN A COOL, DRY PLACE

Megan Terry

This one-act play is a virtuoso piece for three actors. The three
basic characters are a smooth lawyer, his subservient henchman,
and the thug the two had hired to kill the lawyer's wife. They
are now in jail together—but the actors transform out of the
cell and become, at various times, machines, cavalrymen and
Indians, English soldiers at the Jamestown landing, Hollywood
gangsters, and assistants at a Mass. Gregory, the murderer, has,
until this speech, been treated by the other two as an oafish
clown. The audience has felt safe with him. The other two have
just bullied him into relating a sexual dream, and they are now
back in their bunks. Gregory gives the following speech to the
audience. During the course of the speech his character alters
subtly until the audience realizes that they have been the dupes—
their patronizing attitude has been apprehended and the clown
has turned sinister.

The character work should be full (although the decisions of

136

detail are up to the actor), but the character is *telling* a story, not acting it out, and he is telling it to get a certain reaction. To achieve the full effectiveness of the speech the actor should work simply, maintaining contact with the audience in the most direct way. By doing this he can make the end of the speech truly unsettling.

GREGORY (*Alone, he rises from the floor during his speech*): This girl on our street, she used to drink water from the swamp on her way home from school . . . and she swallowed tons of this here water . . . and one day she was swallowing the water and it was loaded with snake eggs and she didn't know it . . . and she swallowed this snake egg . . . BUT SHE DIDN'T KNOW IT . . . and nobody else knew it. Cause everyone just thought it was plain water, but this here snake egg was too small to see, see? And then this girl she got skinnier and skinnier, until she was just bones except for her little belly which was round and tight as a basketball. The last day of her life she was laying on her bed in her bedroom see, and her grandmother was trying to make her eat see, and her Dad was trying to make her eat some of this here soup. And she just stared up at them. She was dead, get it. But they didn't get it yet. And they's all banded about her bed waving these here spoons and dishes . . . and they keep pleading her to eat this good grub and that. Finally, her old man grabs her jaws and forces them open. Guess who sticks a tongue out at him? Yeah. Guess who? Yeah! It was the snake. It was the snake grown up! (*He looks at audience a moment and then becomes withdrawn*) Don't be nice to me. I can't stand that. Don't be nice to me or I'll bite!

AMERICA HURRAH

Jean-Claude van Itallie

Interview, the first of the three plays of *America Hurrah*, is peopled with applicants and interviewers. The former are dingy and apologetic, the latter glib and charming. Halfway through the play the masks dissolve and each of the characters half-enacts, half-relates a story, with the other members of the cast assisting silently. The Third Interviewer is, in this fragment, a vote-seeking politician. The technique of the "I said's" allows him to relate to the audience in one way, to the members of the crowd who approach him, in another. He is supremely self-confident and can be all things to all people, delighting the crowd with his sincerity and the audience with his chicanery. The actor can choose his own accent and characterization as this speech is the politician's only appearance in the play.

ACT I

POLITICIAN: Thank you very much, I said cheerfully, and good luck to you, I said, turning my smile to the next one.

Our children *are* our most important asset, I agreed earnestly. Yes they are, I said solemnly. Children, I said, with a long pause, are our most important asset. I only wish I could, madame, I said earnestly, standing tall, but rats, I said regretfully, are a city matter.

Nobody knows more about red tape than I do, I said knowingly, and I wish you luck, I said, turning my smile to the next one.

I certainly will, I said, with my eyes sparkling, taking a pencil out of my pocket. And what's your name, I said, looking at her sweetly and signing my name at the same time. That's a lovely name, I said.

Yes sir, I said, those were the days. And good luck to you, sir, I said respectfully but heartily, and look out for the curb, I said, turning my smile to the next one.

Indeed yes, the air we breathe *is* foul, I said indignantly.

I agree with you entirely, I said wholeheartedly. And if my opponent wins it's going to get worse, I said with conviction. We'd all die within ten years, I said. And good luck to you, madame, I said politely, and turned my smile to the next one.

Well, I said confidingly, getting a bill through the legislature is easier said than done, answering violence, I said warningly, with violence, I said earnestly, is not the answer, and how do you do I said, turning my smile to the next one.

No, I said, I never said my opponent would kill us all. No, I said, I never said that. May the best man win, I said manfully.

I do feel, I said without false modesty, that I'm better qualified in the field of foreign affairs than my opponents are, yes, I said, *but*, I said, with a pause for emphasis, foreign policy is the business of the President, not the Governor, therefore I will say nothing about the war, I said with finality.

Do you want us shaking hands, I asked the photographer, turning my profile to the left. Goodbye, I said cheerfully, and good luck to you too.

I'm sorry, I said seriously, but I'll have to study that question a good deal more before I can answer it.

Of course, I said frowning, we must all support the President, I said as I turned concernedly to the next one.

I'm sorry about the war, I said. Nobody could be sorrier than I am, I said sorrowfully. But I'm afraid, I said gravely, that there are no easy answers. (*Smiles, pleased with himself*) Good luck to you too, I said cheerfully, and turned my smile to the next one.

COMEDY

THE CRITIC
R. B. Sheridan

The Critic, one of the finest burlesques in the language, appeared in 1779. Its alternative title is *A Tragedy Rehearsed.* In it Sheridan ridicules well-worn stage traditions and the excesses of sentimentality. Mr. Puff, the author of the play that is to be rehearsed, describes his methods of advertising thus: "PUFFING is of various sorts—the principal are, THE PUFF DIRECT—THE PUFF PRELIMINARY—THE PUFF COLLATERAL —THE PUFF COLLUSIVE, and THE PUFF OBLIQUE, or PUFF by IMPLICATION."

In this particular scene, in which he is talking to Sneer and Dangle, he is enlarging on the uses of advertising in drawing money from a gullible public. No one who saw Sir Laurence Olivier in *The Critic* will easily forget his bravura, wit and speed in the part of Puff.

PUFF: Hark'ee!—by advertisements—TO THE CHARITABLE AND HUMANE! and TO THOSE WHOM PROVIDENCE HATH BLESSED WITH AFFLUENCE!
SNEER: Oh, I understand you.
PUFF: And in truth, I deserved what I got! for, I suppose never man went through such a series of calamities in the same space of time. Sir, I was five times made a bankrupt, and reduced from a state of affluence, by a train of unavoidable misfortunes; then, sir, though a very industrious

140

tradesman, I was twice burned out, and lost my little all both times; I lived upon those fires a month. I soon after was confined by a most excruciating disorder, and lost the use of my limbs; that told very well, for I had the case strongly attested, and went about to collect the subscriptions myself.

DANGLE: Egad, I believe that was when you first called on me.

PUFF: In November last?—O no; I was at that time a close prisoner in the Marshalsea, for a debt benevolently contracted to serve a friend—I was afterwards twice tapped for a dropsy, which declined into a very profitable consumption. I was then reduced to—O no—then I became a widow with six helpless children, having had eleven husbands pressed, and being left every time eight months gone with child, and without money to get me into an hospital!

SNEER: And you bore all with patience, I make no doubt?

PUFF: Why yes, though I made some occasional attempts at *felo de se*; but as I did not find those rash actions answer, I left off killing myself very soon. Well, sir, at last, what with bankruptcies, fires, gout, dropsies, imprisonments, and other valuable calamities, having got together a pretty handsome sum, I determined to quit a business which had always gone rather against my conscience, and in a more liberal way still to indulge my talents for fiction and embellishment, through my favourite channels of diurnal communication—and so, sir, you have my history.

Omit Sneer's and Dangle's lines and Puff's "Why yes, though."

DESIGN FOR LIVING

Noel Coward

Noel Coward wrote *Design for Living* for himself and the Lunts. Lynn Fontanne played Gilda, Alfred Lunt Otto, a painter, and Coward himself Leo, a writer. Before the play opens both men were in love with Gilda, but she chose to live with Otto. In his introduction to *Play Parade* in which *Design for Living* appears, Coward says, "I never intended for a moment that the design for living suggested in the play should apply to anyone outside its three principal characters, Gilda, Otto, and Leo. These glib, over-articulate, and amoral creatures force their lives into fantastic shapes and problems because they cannot help themselves. Impelled chiefly by the impact of their personalities each upon the other, they are like moths in a pool of light, unable to tolerate the lonely outer darkness, and equally unable to share the light without colliding constantly and bruising one another's wings."

The play is set in Otto's shabby studio in Paris where he and Gilda are living. It is about ten o'clock on a spring morning. A picture dealer friend, Ernest, arrives with a Matisse which he has just acquired. Gilda tells him that Otto is still asleep having been awake all night with a bad attack of neuralgia. In the course of conversation, Ernest says that Leo has arrived back from the States the evening before. He is now wealthy and is staying at the George V. Suddenly Otto walks in; he has unexpectedly returned from Bordeaux where he has been painting a portrait. Gilda tells him that Leo is back and urges him and Ernest to go round to the George V while she tidies up. No sooner have they left, than the bedroom door opens and Leo, who has spent the night in the studio, appears. He and Gilda are both concerned about Otto's reaction to what has happened, but at the moment when Otto returns they both happen to be laughing helplessly about an incident from the past, when Leo pushed Otto into a bath and turned the water on him. The scene which contains the following explosion from Otto ends Act I.

ACT I

OTTO (*furiously*): Well, one thing that magnificent outburst has done for me is this: I don't feel shut out any more. Do you hear? Not any more! And I'm extremely grateful to you. You were right about me being hurt and grieved. I was. But that's over, too. I've seen something in you that I've never seen before; in all these years I've never noticed it—I never realized that, deep down underneath your superficial charm and wit, you're nothing but a cheap, second-rate little opportunist, ready to sacrifice anything, however sacred, to the excitement of the moment—

GILDA: Otto! Otto—listen a minute; please listen—

OTTO (*turning to her*): Listen to what? A few garbled explanations and excuses, fully charged with a hundred per cent feminine emotionalism, appealing to me to hold on to reason and intelligence as it's "our only chance." I don't want an "only chance"—I don't want a chance to do anything but say what I have to say and leave you both to your own goddamned devices! Where was this much vaunted reason and intelligence last night? Working overtime, I'm sure. Working in a hundred small female ways. I expect your reason and intelligence prompted you to wear your green dress, didn't it? With the emerald earrings? And your green shoes, too, although they hurt you when you dance. Reason must have whispered kindly in your ear on your way back here in the taxi. It must have said, "Otto's in Bordeaux, and Bordeaux is a long way away, so everything will be quite safe!" That's reason, all right—pure reason—

GILDA (*collapsing at the table*): Stop it! Stop it! How can you be so cruel? How can you say such vile things?

OTTO (*without a break*): I hope "intelligence" gave you a little extra jab and suggested that you lock the door? In furtive underhand affairs doors are always locked—

LEO: Shut up, Otto. What's the use of going on like that?

143

OTTO: Don't speak to me—old, old Loyal Friend that you are! Don't speak to me, even if you have the courage, and keep out of my sight from now onwards—
LEO: Bravo, Deathless Drama!
OTTO: Wrong again. Lifeless Comedy. You've set me free from a stale affection that must have died ages ago without my realizing it. Go ahead, my boy, and do great things! You've already achieved a Hotel de Luxe, a few smart suits, and the woman I loved. Go ahead, maybe there are still higher peaks for you to climb. Good luck, both of you! Wonderful luck! I wish you were dead and in hell! (*He slams out of the room as the curtain falls*)

Omit Gilda's and Leo's lines.

THE IRREGULAR VERB TO LOVE
Hugh and Margaret Williams

Hedda Rankin's husband is a zoo official. They live with their children, Andrew and Lucy, in a maisonette opposite the zoo in Regent's Park. Hedda is devoted to animals and gets herself involved in campaigns on their behalf; she has just finished a spell in prison. This scene, at the beginning of the play, occurs just before Hedda returns to her family. Her son, Andrew, who has just hitch-hiked through Europe, has arrived with a Greek girl who speaks no English.

   He is extroverted, casual, long-haired, bearded, sunburned, and dirty. In this speech he is describing his mother to Michael, a friend of his sister.

ACT I
ANDREW: Has Lucy told you she once visited every casbah from Casablanca to Algiers trying to make the Arabs kinder

to their animals? She used to demonstrate how to bathe their dogs and remove their ticks. She washed them in the streets and in the souks. In a tin tub, Bob Martin's Bloom shampoo. The filthy dogs hated it and the Arabs laughed their heads off. Lucy? (*Gives her a packet of cigarettes, hands the other packet to MICHAEL*) Try one? Then she'd empty the dirty water, put her tin tub back in the car, and drive off to the next place. She was, of course, eventually bitten.

(*MICHAEL has opened cigarettes. ANDREW crosses to him*) According to her the dog only bit her because it had soap in its eye, but the authorities insisted it was mad, had it destroyed and she was flown to the Pasteur Institute in Paris for injections against rabies.

(*ANDREW helps himself to cigarette from MICHAEL'S packet*) That was to get rid of her, of course. My father flew out and eventually brought her home, but not before she'd been desperately ill because she proved allergic to the injections. It was all very expensive and they couldn't afford a holiday for two years. I'm always so thankful I'm her son and not her husband. Poor Papa, he's spent a lot of time fetching her back from places. First the casbah, now the clink.

(*There is a sound of hooting from a car off-stage L. ANDREW moves to the window*) Sounds as if he's just completed his latest mission.

(*ANDREW goes through lower window on to the balcony*) Hullo! Welcome home!

THE LESSON

Eugene Ionesco

When this one-act play was produced at the Arts Theatre in 1955 it marked Ionesco's first appearance in the West End of London. It is described as a comic drama and the playwright gives a clear indication as to how the actor playing the professor should look: "a little old man with a pointed white beard; he wears pince-nez and a black skullcap, a long black schoolmaster's gown, a white stiff collar and tie." He also describes his manner as "excessively polite, very shy, a voice subdued by his timidity, very correct, very professorial. He is constantly rubbing his hands together, now and again a prurient gleam, quickly dismissed, lights up his eyes. In the course of the drama his timidity will slowly and imperceptibly disappear; the prurient gleam in his eyes will end by blazing into an insistent, lecherous, devouring flame." The actor should note that this particular scene comes not quite halfway through the play.

The action takes place in the professor's study which is also his dining room.

THE PROFESSOR: Summing-up, then: learning to pronounce takes years and years. Thanks to science, we can do it in a few minutes. In order to make sounds and words and anything you like, you must realize then that the air has to be pitilessly forced out of the lungs and then made to pass gently over the vocal cords, lightly brushing them, so that like harps or leaves beneath the wind, they suddenly start quivering, trembling, vibrating, vibrating, vibrating or hissing, or rustling, or bristling, or whistling—(*He circles table and couch*) and with a whistle set everything in motion— (*The PUPIL rises and follows the PROFESSOR to R*)— uvula, tongue, palate, teeth—
PUPIL: I've got toothache.
PROFESSOR:—lips. (*He circles the table*) Finally words come out through the nose, the mouth, the ears, the pores

146

of the skin, bringing in their train all the uprooted organs of speech we've just named, a powerful, majestic swarm, no less than what we improperly call the voice—(*He crosses down R*) modulating in song or rising in terrible symphonic wrath, a regular procession, sheaves of assorted blossoms, of sonorous conceits, labials, dentals, plosives, palatals and the rest, some soft and gentle—(*He crosses to L of the PUPIL*) some harsh and violent.

PUPIL (*sitting on the couch at the downstage end*): Yes, sir. I've got toothache.

PROFESSOR: We go on. We go on. As for the neo-Spanish languages, they are such very near relations that we might almost think of them as second cousins. Moreover, they have the same mother—Spanish. The *H* is unaspirated. That is why it is so difficult to tell one from the other. That is why it helps so much to pronounce properly, to avoid mistakes in pronunciation. Pronunciation is in itself worth a whole dialect. Bad pronunciation can play you some funny tricks. Allow me, while we're on the subject, to tell you a little personal story, in parenthesis. (*There is a slight relaxation. He sits above the PUPIL on the couch and for a moment gives himself up to his memories. His expression becomes sentimental, but he quickly recovers himself*) It was when I was very young, little more than a child, perhaps. I was doing my military service. I had a friend in the regiment, a viscount, who had a rather serious speech defect— he was unable to pronounce the letter *f*. Instead of saying *f*, he used to say *f*. If we wanted to say "fresh fields and pastures new," he would say "fresh fields and pastures new." He pronounced *filly* as *filly*; he said *Franklin* instead of *Franklin*; *fimblerigger* instead of *fimblerigger*; *fiddlesticks* instead of *fiddlesticks*; *funny face* instead of *funny face*. *Fe Fi Fo Fum* instead of "I smell the blood of an Englishman"; *Philip* instead of *Philip*; *fictory* instead of *fictory*; *February* instead of *February*; *April-May* instead of *April-May*; *Galeries*

Lafayette and not, as it should be pronounced, *Galeries La-fayette*; *Napoleon* instead of *Napoleon*; *etcetera* instead of *etcetera* and so on, etcetera—only he was lucky enough to be able to conceal the defect so well, thanks to his choice of hats, that no one ever noticed it.

Omit the pupil's lines.

THE LOVE OF FOUR COLONELS
Peter Ustinov

The scene is the office of the Allied Military Administration set up in a village in the Hartz Mountains, immediately after the Second World War. The colonels appointed by Britain, France, America and Russia are chatting in their rooms, when suddenly a mysterious man arrives. He is tall, thin and smiling and dressed as a tramp. He says he has an appointment to see them. They are unaware of this but when he asks them to check it in their appointment book, they find—unaccountably—that his name is there.

When challenged to produce a satisfactory permit, he starts searching for one, but produces instead, first a scroll which turns out to be a "permission from Nero to taunt the lions before their dinner of gospelers" and next "a front row ticket for Robespierre's execution."

The note of fantasy is heightened when, at the end of the act, on being asked by the French colonel who he is, he replies "Me? Silly boy, I'm the Wicked Fairy."

ACT I

The figure of a MAN appears silently at the door, dressed as a tramp. He is very tall, thin, and he smiles.

MAN (*searching in his vast coat*): You really are most difficult to convince. What's this? (*He pulls out a scroll*) Oh, no. This is permission from Nero to taunt the lions before their dinner of gospelers. Here we are. No. A front-row ticket for Robespierre's execution. A disappointing affair. The weather was far from perfect. There's a special kind of weather which is ideal for executions, you know—you need an autumn morning, really, to surround the scene with an aura of poetic melancholy, and just enough of an orange sun to catch the blade. For lions, on the other hand, you can't do better than your mid-summer heat, in which the poor beasts are torn between an oppressive lethargy and their greed for blood. Such leonine quandaries drag out the agony of the gospelers deliciously. (*With a giggle*) But what am I doing, talking about it as though it still went on today. No, alas. (*He sighs*) The taste for limited horror was dissipated. A decadence set in. Our love of quality was polluted by a love of quantity. Nowadays we do things on a majestic scale, with guns and bombs and gasses, and it's surprising how the human species obeys our every whim in this respect. . . . (*looking at the colonels*) All dressed up in their little boiler suits, with bits of gold and silver braid to mark the degree of their guilt. (*He laughs*) Oh dear, oh dear. . . .

THE PROPOSAL

Anton Chekhov, *translated by Elisaveta Fen*

The Proposal was described by Chekhov as a jest in one act: "A scabby little vaudeville which I've scratched out for the provinces." It is farcical in style.

The setting is the drawing room in a wealthy landowner's

(Choobukov's) house. Here he lives with his daughter, Natalyia Stepanovna, aged twenty-five. She is unmarried. Lomov, a neighboring landowner, calls to see them. He is described as "healthy, well-nourished but hypochondriacal." Chekhov draws this character with humor, tolerance and affection.

Lomov has arrived resplendent in evening dress and white gloves to ask for Natalyia's hand. Choobukov is overjoyed and rushes out to tell his daughter.

Left on the stage alone, Lomov speaks these lines.

LOMOV (*alone*): I'm cold . . . I'm trembling all over as if I were going in for an examination. The main thing is to make up your mind. If you think too long, keep talking and hesitating and waiting for the ideal woman or for real true love, you'll never get married. Brr! . . . I'm cold! Natalyia Stepanovna is an excellent housekeeper, educated, not bad-looking. . . . What more do I want? But I'm in such a state that I'm beginning to have noises in my head. . . . (*Drinks water*) Yet I mustn't stay single. In the first place, I'm thirty-five already—a critical age, so to speak. Secondly, I must have an ordered, regular life. . . . I've got a heart disease, with continual palpitations. . . . I flare up so easily, and I'm always getting terribly agitated. . . . Even now my lips are trembling and my right eyelid's twitching. . . . But the worst thing is my sleep. No sooner do I get into bed and start dropping off to sleep than something stabs me in my left side. Stab! And it goes right through my shoulder to my head. . . . I jump up like a madman, walk about for a bit and lie down again. . . . But directly I start dozing off, there it goes again in my side—stab! And the same thing happens twenty times over. . . .

THE PUBLIC EYE

Peter Shaffer

This play was first presented in a double bill with *The Private Ear*. This telephone conversation comes at the end of the play. Charles, Belinda's staid husband, has sensed that she has become indifferent to him and suspects that there may be another man involved. He employs an agency to check up on her and Julian Christoferou is the detective they send to shadow her. Although neither speaks to the other, Belinda and Julian develop an understanding and for three weeks they spend their days cinema-going and sight-seeing around London, one day one giving the lead, another day the other. Belinda confesses what has been happening to Charles, unaware that it is he who has employed Julian. When the truth comes out, Julian helps the couple toward a better relationship. He instructs Belinda to go off in an apparent rage and then tells Charles to adopt the role of detective and follow her. He assures Charles that he will handle his clients' accounts for him while he is away from his office and when a client, at that moment, telephones, Julian takes the call confidently.

Julian Christoferou is an eccentric character who has a great deal of wit. The part calls for technical virtuosity and verve.

JULIAN (*He sits at the desk. Into the telephone*): Well, permit me to introduce myself. My name is Christoferou. Julian Christoferou. Diplomas in accountancy from the Universities of Beirut and Damascus. Author of the well-known handbook *Teach Yourself Tax Evasion*. What seems to be your particular problem? . . . Fifteen thousand pounds Schedule A. Seventeen thousand pounds Schedule D. It's monstrous! You haven't paid it, I hope? I'm delighted to hear it. . . . Of course not. Paying any tax that is over five per cent of your total income I consider a desperate imprudence. . . . Yes, of course, we have limitless experience in this field. Christoferou and Sidley. A firm of the very highest . . . (*He takes a spoonful of grapefruit and pulls a face at its bitter taste. He picks up the sugar canister and sprinkles the fruit, but it is empty. He bangs it to shake the sugar loose, but to no avail*) I think you'd better come round and see me immediately. . . . No, my dear sir, I assure you, we won't let the government touch a penny piece of your money. Not without a battle that would make fifteen thousand pounds Schedule D. Seventeen thousand pounds Schedule B. It's monstrous! You haven't paid it? Come round in, shall we say, one hour? . . . Excellent. I look forward to it. In the meantime, don't worry about a thing. And if you could bring round with you a pound of granulated sugar, I'd be greatly obliged. Good day to you, sir . . . good day! (*He replaces the receiver as the curtain falls*)

THE REHEARSAL

Jean Anouilh, *translated by*
Pamela Hansford Johnson and Kitty Black

The play is set in modern times in an eighteenth-century castle. The count and countess are rehearsing, in costume, a play by Marivaux. Among the players is a young nursemaid, Lucile, with whom the count (Tiger) falls in love.

Another of his guests, his friend Hero—a forty-year-old libertine and drunkard—is jealously concerned at the depth of the count's emotion for Lucile.

In the hopes of breaking the count's hold on Lucile's imagination, the countess persuades Hero to try to seduce Lucile and she arranges for a telegram to be sent to Tiger calling him away that evening.

The speech given here is taken from the third act of the play which is set in Lucile's attic bedroom in the west wing. Hero enters, still in costume and says to her, "Don't be afraid. Tiger's just telephoned to say he won't be back till late tonight. He asked me to give you the message and keep you company for a while." He then proceeds to try to disillusion her about the strength and sincerity of the count's love, telling her that the count has decided to go away. Hero now woos her himself and at the end of the scene he is holding her in his arms.

ACT III

HERO (*smiling*): You realize he's already rather late? We have plenty of time. . . . The butler and the cook are getting drunk in the pantry and I've packed the paratrooper off to do the same in the next village. All the others are shut up in their rooms, miles away in the other wing, wondering what's going to happen next. I can see them tossing on their beds. Monsieur Damiens, hairy and dark as a fat crow who's lost his piece of cheese; Hortensia and the countess in their silks and satins, with detective stories and sleeping pills within reach. But sleep stays away! What about the little plotter in her attic in the west wing, cooking up God knows what against the family concord and the approved liaisons. Won't someone manage to get rid of her at last? (*He takes a step*) My dear, Tiger has suddenly realized, too late, that he has made a great mistake, the sort of mistake only he can make. If he had asked my advice beforehand, I would have told him to spare you this unhappiness. You were a virgin, virginity was your meager capital—he should never have touched it. Besides, there's something about you. I would have said to him, you can do as you please with a chambermaid, that goes without saying; if you don't have her the footman will, either today or the day after. You're worth more than that; I admit it. But don't be too angry with him, all the same. He isn't wicked. He's a sentimentalist, an incurable sentimentalist, and it goes to his head—that's all. Besides he has every excuse. . . . It's so adorable, a new little being nestling in your arms, saying she loves you, that she belongs to you for ever. For ever—for you that

153

meant tonight—the here and now. It was a brand-new pleasure for him, something he's never known before. He'd have to be very high-minded to tear his arms away, to say no! And besides, as you've just told me, it's a risk all girls have to run. After all, if they ask for it. . . . The trouble is that next morning, you find the little one still loves you. "For ever" so far as she's concerned begins with break- fast. And now you have to start worrying about her. She's deep in confidences already. The little darling, head on your shoulder, has already started to prattle about her old mother, who's so lonely, to whom one must be so very kind—of the little dishes she cooks so nicely, the name she's going to give her first baby. It's all gone, the unique joy of the night before, your sacrificial fawn. Hey presto! You're carrying the slop pail for the entire family! You can see yourself, already, pushing the pram. . . . A free translation, of course. I know that you were sensible and discreet. I'll go on working just the same; he'll never buy me anything; we shall be free; nothing will matter but our love. . . . Shall I tell you the whole truth, my dear? Yes. You're strong enough to bear it now. That's what frightened Tiger. He would rather you'd asked him for a mink coat and a nicely furnished little flat. To have a nice little mistress, in a life like his, that fits in very nicely. A great unselfish love—that is beyond price.

LUCILE: Why didn't he tell me himself?

HERO: Why should you make a hero out of that likable playboy? He knows, like all of us, that there's only one cure for love—flight. He has flown.

Omit Lucile's line.

VERSE PLAYS

AS YOU LIKE IT

William Shakespeare

Adam is one of the most endearing of the smaller parts in Shakespeare's plays. For many years he was servant to Sir Rowland de Boys but he now serves Oliver, his eldest son. However, he is much more attached to Orlando, Oliver's younger brother. When Orlando defeats Charles, Duke Frederick's wrestler, Oliver is consumed with jealousy and hatred of his brother. At the beginning of the scene from which Adam's speech is chosen Adam tells Orlando that Oliver means

> "To burn the lodging where you use to lie,
> And you within it. If he fail of that,
> He will have other means to cut you off;"

Adam then urges Orlando to escape and offers to give him his life savings of five hundred crowns and go with him. Adam is nearly eighty and in this speech Shakespeare paints a touching picture of the old man's courage and loyalty.

ACT II, SCENE iii

ADAM: I have five hundred crowns,
    The thrifty hire I saved under your father,
    Which I did store to be my foster-nurse
    When service should in my old limbs lie lame
    And unregarded age in corners thrown:
    Take that; and He that doth the ravens feed,
    Yea, providently caters for the sparrow,

Be comfort to my age! Here is the gold;
All this I give you. Let me be your servant:
Though I look old, yet I am strong and lusty:
For in my youth I never did apply
Hot and rebellious liquors in my blood,
Nor did not with unbashful forehead woo
The means of weakness and debility;
Therefore my age is as a lusty winter,
Frosty, but kindly: let me go with you;
I'll do the service of a younger man
In all your business and necessities.
ORLANDO: O good old man, how well in thee appears
The constant service of the antique world,
When service sweat for duty, not for meed!
Thou art not for the fashion of these times,
Where none will sweat but for promotion,
And having that, do choke their service up
Even with the having: it is not so with thee.
But, poor old man, thou prunest a rotten tree,
That cannot so much as a blossom yield
In lieu of all thy pains and husbandry.
But come thy ways: we'll go along together;
And ere we have thy youthful wages spent,
We'll light upon some settled low content.
ADAM: Master, go on, and I will follow thee,
To the last gasp, with truth and loyalty.
From seventeen years till now almost fourscore
Here lived I, but now live here no more.
At seventeen years many their fortunes seek;
But at fourscore it is too late a week:
Yet fortune cannot recompense me better
Than to die well and not my master's debtor.
(*Exeunt*)

Omit Orlando's lines.

156

CHRISTOPHER COLUMBUS

Louis MacNeice

Louis MacNeice wrote this radio play to order to celebrate the four hundred and fiftieth anniversary of the discovery of America. In it he tells the story of the early struggles of Columbus in Portugal and later in Spain to get ships and money for his expedition to discover land in the west. Finally, after two Royal Commissions have rejected him and his ideas, he wins the support of Queen Isabella of Castile who promises him three ships. Columbus and his crew of ex-jailbirds succeed in discovering a new world and return to Spain in triumph. He delivers this speech to King Ferdinand and Queen Isabella at the court of Barcelona. Columbus is now no longer a young man; the year is 1493.

COLUMBUS: Your Catholic Majesties . . . It is hard for me
On such a day and before such an audience,
Feeling myself on a pinnacle high among clouds of
dream,
To find the words—it is hard to find the words
For a theme that no man yet has phrased or painted—
The passage where no passage lay,
The world where no world was before.
But this is what I have done:
I took three ships, and sailed them into the teeth of the
West,
Into what seemed the certainty of death
And against the veto of Nature.
Weeks went by and no land came, I might have
Well turned back, but I did not, I went on,
And in the ripeness of God's will I found
The Second Earthly Paradise and there
I raised the cross of Christ and the banner of Castile.
Your Majesties, look out yonder,
Look out yonder along the line of my arm

157

Across Tibidabo and the hills of Spain:
Four thousand miles out there to the west
Lie uncharted lands—they are yours to chart,
Uncounted treasure—yours for the taking,
Aye and countless hordes of heathen men
Who are from now your subjects,
Unenlightened souls who wait the light.
Aye, your Majesties, this new world
That I have opened up through the will of God—
Only God can tell what is its total worth,
And God alone knows what it will become
Or what may be the blessings that late or soon
May flow from thence to Europe—
Aye, and to all mankind from this new world.
This is my story and this is what it means:
Here and now at your court in Barcelona
In the year of Our Lord
Fourteen-Hundred-And-Ninety-Three,
Before the Throne of Spain and the eyes and ears of
Europe
And before the crowded jury of posterity—
I have brought you a new world.

CYRANO DE BERGERAC

Edmond Rostand, *translated by Humbert Wolfe*

Cyrano de Bergerac was written in 1898. It is a mingling of
panache, lyric, love and stage craftsmanship which must in-
evitably lose a great deal in translation. Humbert Wolfe's
version is preferred here because it attempts to capture the sheer,

fragile poetry of Rostand's rhymed couplets and the triumphant click as the rhymes fall into their places. Rostand dedicated his play thus

> "It was to the soul of CYRANO that
> I intended to dedicate this poem.
> But since that soul has been reborn
> in you, COQUELIN, it is to you that I
> dedicate it." E.R.

The first four acts take place in 1640; the fifth, from which this scene is taken, in 1655. When the play opens, Christian de Neuvillette has come to Paris to join the Guards. He is passionately in love with Roxane, but although he is handsome, he is inarticulate and quite incapable of declaring his love. She is also loved by her cousin, Cyrano—the most accomplished swordsman of the day—who is disfigured in his own eyes by an enormous nose. Roxane and Cyrano meet at the Bakery of the Poets and she tells him that she is in love with Christian but that he will not speak to her. She begs Cyrano to look after him and to prevent him from fighting duels. Cyrano agrees and when next he and Christian meet he persuades him to repeat to Roxane the eloquent words of love he gives him each day. The result is that Roxane is wooed by Cyrano's words spoken by Christian. Roxane and Christian are married secretly and shortly afterwards the regiment leaves for Arras. Christian is killed in the battle.

The final act is set in the Park of the Convent of the Ladies of the Cross in Paris. It is autumn. Every Saturday for the past ten years Cyrano has come to visit Roxane, who is living in the convent, to give her news of the outside world. This particular Saturday, as Cyrano is coming out of his door, a lackey in an upstairs window lets fall a heavy log of wood onto his head. Cyrano nevertheless comes to see Roxane as usual, his heavily bandaged head concealed under his hat. He gives Roxane the latest "gazette." Roxane discovers, during the scene, that Christian was Cyrano's mouthpiece, that his was the soul that she loved and still loves. The lines that follow are spoken during Cyrano's final duel with death.

ACT IV

CYRANO: But I must go, forgive me. They are calling,
     And for an escort, see! the moonbeams falling.
(*To ROXANE*)
     I would not have you cease to mourn your lover
     Christian, the good, the fair; but when all's over,
     And the great cold has clapped me, body and sense,
     do on your mourning with a difference,
     and in his weeds give me at least a share.
ROXANE: I swear.
CYRANO (*shaken by a great agony, rises with a sudden*):
     Not here!
     I say, not in this chair.
(*They run to him*)
     Off, all of you! I'll wait by this tree rooted.
(*Silence*)
     Death comes. Already I'm with marble booted
     and gloved with lead; but, as she comes, I'll stand
     thus to attention with my sword in hand.
LE BRET: Cyrano.
(*All draw back horror-stricken*)
CYRANO: Death's nose is snub, therefore she quizzes mine.
     On guard, you drab!
(*Draws his sword*)
     What say you? It is useless! Well I know it.
     It is the hope forlorn that seals the poet.
     The desperate venture still rewards us most.
     But what is this innumerable host?
     I know them by the devil in their eyes.
     Have at you, falsehood, that for compromise!
     Prejudice, craven fear, you seek for terms?
     Here is my sword! Go ask them of the worms!
     But now my victor overtops the rest.
     Salute stupidity! Here is my breast!
(*He makes huge passes with his sword and stands gasping*)

You have taken all—the laurel and the rose.
Take them. There is a secret my heart owes
in your despite, and when my feet have trod
tonight the azure ante-rooms of God,
What I bring home unstained with gold will splash
the basalt floors.

(*He lunges with the sword*)
It is

ROXANE (*bending over him and kissing his forehead*):
What?

CYRANO (*opening his eyes, recognizes her and says wearily*):
My panache.

Omit Roxane's lines and Le Bret's line.

DR. FAUSTUS

Christopher Marlowe

The Tragedy of Dr. Faustus was written between 1587 and 1593. Marlowe based his play on the German legend of the magician who sacrificed his soul to the devil in order to gain universal knowledge and power.

In the first scene, we find Faustus in his study restless and impatient of the limits of human intelligence. He succeeds in conjuring up Mephistopheles by black magic, and tells him that he wishes to surrender his soul to Lucifer on the condition that he is given Mephistopheles as his servant, sworn to obey his commands, for twenty-four years.

At midnight Mephistopheles returns to Faustus and tells him that his master Lucifer has agreed to the bargain.

In the middle scenes of the play we see Faustus exercising his powers. The writing here is uneven, but in the magnificent scene at the end of the play Faustus' agony of mind is described in one of the most moving and splendid speeches that Marlowe ever wrote. At the beginning of the speech, the sands are running out and Faustus has "but one bare hour to live." At the end of it, the clock strikes twelve and the stage direction reads "Exeunt Devils with Faustus."

ACT V, SCENE ii

(*The clock strikes eleven*)
FAUSTUS: Ah, Faustus,
  Now hast thou but one bare hour to live,
  And then thou must be damn'd perpetually!
  Stand still, you ever-moving spheres of heaven,
  That time may cease, and midnight never come;
  Faire Nature's eye, rise, rise again, and make
  Perpetual day; or let this hour be but
  A year, a month, a week, a natural day,
  That Faustus may repent and save his soul!
  O lente, lente, currite, noctis equi!
  The stars move still, time runs, the clock will strike,
  The devil will come, and Faustus must be damn'd.
  O, I'll leap up to my God!—who pulls me down?
  See, see, where Christ's blood streams in the firmament!
  One drop would save my soul, half a drop: ah, my Christ!
  Yet will I call on him: O, spare me, Lucifer!—
  Where is it now? 'tis gone! and see where God
  Stretcheth out his arm, and bends his ireful brows!
  Mountains and hills, come, come and fall on me,
  And hide me from the heavy wrath of God!
  No, no!
  Then will I headlong run into the earth:
  Earth, gape! O, no, it will not harbour me!
  You stars that reign'd at my nativity,
  Whose influence hath allotted death and hell,
  Now draw up Faustus, like a foggy mist,

Into the entrails of yon lab'ring cloud
That, when you vomit forth into the air,
My limbs may issue from your smoky mouths,
So that my soul may but ascend to heaven!
(*The clock strikes*)
Ah, half the hour is past! 'twill·all be passed anon.
O God,
If thou wilt not have mercy on my soul,
Yet for Christ's sake, whose blood hath ransom'd me,
Impose some end to my incessant pain:
Let Faustus live in hell a thousand years,
A hundred thousand, and at last be sav'd!
O, no end is limited to damned souls!
Why wert thou not a creature wanting soul?
Or why is this immortal that thou hast?
Ah, Pythagoras' metempsychosis, were that true,
This soul should fly from me, and I be changed
Unto some brutish beast! all beasts are happy,
For, when they die,
Their souls are soon dissolved in elements;
But mine must live still to be plagued in hell.
Curs'd be the parents that engender'd me!
No, Faustus, curse thyself, curse Lucifer
That hath depriv'd thee of the joys of heaven.
(*The clock strikes twelve*)
O, it strikes, it strikes! Now, body, turn to air,
Or Lucifer will bear thee quick to hell!
O soul be changed into little water-drops,
And fall into the ocean, ne'er be found!
(*Thunder and enter the Devils*)
My God, my God, look not so fierce on me!
Adders and serpents, let me breathe a while!
Ugly hell, gape not! come not, Lucifer!
I'll burn my books!—Ah, Mephistopheles!
(*Exeunt Devils with Faustus*)

163

EVERYMAN

These lines of the Messenger open the famous morality play *Everyman*. The play is believed by some to be the English version by an unknown author of a Dutch original. God sends Death to summon Everyman to make his final journey. Everyman is in the midst of his worldly pleasures. He asks for time to be allowed to gather together friends to travel with him. Friendship, Kindred and Goods all refuse to go with him and only Good Deeds whom he has long neglected eventually accompanies him to the grave. Finally, Everyman dies, shriven of his sins.

Professor Legouis says of this play, "In a sense every dramatic work whether ancient or modern seems frivolous by the side of this essential tragedy."

It is the function of the Messenger in these lines to arrest the attention of the audience and to prepare them for the play. The speech typically points the moral of the tale.

MESSENGER: I pray you all, give your audience,
 And hear this matter with reverence,
 By figure a moral play;
 The Summoning of Everyman called it is,
 That of our lives and ending shows,
 How transitory we be all day:
 This matter is wonderous precious,
 But the intent of it is more gracious,
 And sweet to bear away.
 The story saith: man, in the beginning
 Look well, and take good heed to the ending,
 Be you never so gay.
 Ye think sin in the beginning full sweet,
 Which in the end causeth thy soul to weep.
 When the body lieth in clay.
 Here shall you see how Fellowship and Jollity,
 Both Strength, Pleasure, and Beauty,

Will fade from thee as flower in May;
For ye shall hear, how our Heavenly King
Calleth Everyman to a general reckoning:
Give audience, and hear what he doth say.

HAMLET

William Shakespeare

Although this is not the most famous of Hamlet's soliloquies, it provides tremendous scope for the actor because it reveals the way in which Hamlet's mind works. Gertrude has told Claudius, Hamlet's uncle and the murderer of his father, that Hamlet has killed Polonius who was concealed behind an arras in her room during a meeting between her and the prince. Claudius, realizing the danger he himself is in, sends Hamlet to England ostensibly to save him from the consequences of the murder of Polonius, but really to encompass his death. On the way to embark, Hamlet sees Fortinbras's Norwegian army marching against Poland. When he questions a captain about the reason for the campaign, he is told

> We go to gain a little patch of ground
> That hath in it no profit but the name.
> To pay five ducats, five, I would not farm it;

Hamlet sees in this incident an incitement to spur him to avenge his father's murder. He feels the contrast between the determination of these men to fight for a worthless plot of land and his own indecision when faced with a much greater motive.

ACT IV, SCENE iv

HAMLET: How all occasions do inform against me,
    And spur my dull revenge! What is a man,

165

If his chief good and market of his time
Be but to sleep and feed? a beast, no more.
Sure, he that made us with such large discourse,
Looking before and after, gave us not
That capability and godlike reason
To fust in us unused. Now, whether it be
Bestial oblivion, or some craven scruple
Of thinking too precisely on th' event,—
A thought which, quarter'd, hath but one part wisdom
And ever three parts coward,—I do not know
Why yet I live to say "This thing's to do";
Sith I have cause, and will, and strength, and means
To do't. Examples, gross as earth, exhort me:
Witness this army, of such mass and charge,
Led by a delicate and tender prince;
Whose spirit, with divine ambition puff'd
Makes mouths at the invisible event;
Exposing what is mortal and unsure
To all that fortune, death, and danger dare,
Even for an egg-shell. Rightly to be great
Is not to stir without great argument,
But greatly to find quarrel in a straw
When honour's at the stake. How stand I, then,
That have a father kill'd, a mother stain'd,
Excitements of my reason and my blood,
And let all sleep? while, to my shame, I see
The imminent death of twenty thousand men,
That for a fantasy and trick of fame
Go to their graves like beds; fight for a plot
Whereon the numbers cannot try the cause,
Which is not tomb enough and continent
To hide the slain?—O, from this time forth,
My thoughts be bloody, or be nothing worth!
(*Exit*)

KING HENRY IV, PART I

William Shakespeare

Hotspur has defeated the Scots in battle and, it is alleged, has taken prisoners which he has kept for himself, sending the King only the Earl of Fife. Accordingly, Henry IV has sent for Hotspur to explain what he has done. At the beginning of this scene, the Earl of Northumberland intercedes for his son and explains that the facts about the prisoners have been misrepresented to the King. At this point the impetuous Hotspur adds his own explanation.

When playing this part one has to remember that Hotspur suffered from an impediment of speech, particularly when he was excited, as he is now. His wife, Lady Percy, says of him that he was the idol of the youth of England. All the young men imitated his mannerisms, his walk

> And speaking thick, which nature made his blemish,
> Became the accents of the valiant.

It is important that this trait not be overdone by the actor in a kind of willful goonery. In this particular speech, certain words seem to lend themselves to faulty articulation. This should underline both Hotspur's character and the comedy element in the speech. For example, the letter *p* in the words *perfumed, pouncet-box, popinjay* and *parmaceti* might be stuttered and these four words should be sufficient to convey the desired effect.

ACT I, SCENE iii

HOTSPUR: My liege, I did deny no prisoners.
But I remember, when the fight was done,
When I was dry with rage and extreme toil,
Breathless and faint, leaning upon my sword,
Came there a certain lord, neat, and trimly dress'd
Fresh as a bridegroom; and his chin new reapt
Show'd like a stubble-land at harvest-home;
He was perfumed like a milliner;
And 'twixt his finger and his thumb he held

167

A pouncet-box, which ever and anon
He gave his nose, and took't away again;—
Who therewith angry, when it next came there,
Took it in snuff:—and still he smiled and talk'd,
And as the soldiers bore dead bodies by,
He call'd them untaught knaves, unmannerly,
To bring a slovenly unhandsome corse
Betwixt the wind and his nobility.
With many holiday and lady terms
He question'd me; amongst the rest, demanded
My prisoners in your majesty's behalf.
I then, all smarting with my wounds being cold,
To be so pester'd with a popinjay,
Out of my grief and my impatience,
Answer'd neglectingly, I know not what,—
He should, or he should not; for he made me mad
To see him shine so brisk, and smell so sweet,
And talk so like a waiting-gentlewoman
Of guns and drums and wounds,—God save the mark!—
And telling me the sovereign'st thing on earth
Was parmaceti for an inward bruise;
And that it was great pity, so it was,
This villainous salt-petre should be digg'd
Out of the bowels of the harmless earth,
Which many a good tall fellow had destroy'd
So cowardly; and but for these vile guns,
He would himself have been a soldier.
This bald unjointed chat of his, my lord,
I answer'd indirectly, as I said;
And I beseech you, let not his report
Come current for an accusation
Betwixt my love and your high majesty.

KING JOHN

William Shakespeare

At the beginning of the play the king of France has demanded, in the name of Prince Arthur, whose cause he is supporting, the whole of England, Ireland, Poitiers, Anjou, Touraine and Maine. King John defies him. When the French ambassador has left, Robert Faulconbridge and his half-brother, Philip, come before the king to settle the disposition of their inheritance. Philip the Bastard is created Sir Richard Plantagenet after his natural father, Richard Cœur-de-Lion, and goes to France with King John.

After negotiations in France, King John creates Prince Arthur duke of Bretagne and earl of Richmond and at the end of this scene of negotiated peace, the Bastard is left alone on the stage and delivers this soliloquy on the subject of commodity or profit.

ACT II, SCENE ii

BASTARD: Mad world! mad kings, mad composition!
    John, to stop Arthur's title in the whole,
    Hath willingly departed with a part;
    And France,—whose armour conscience buckled on,
    Whom zeal and charity brought to the field
    As God's own soldier,—rounded in the ear
    With that same purpose-changer, that sly devil;
    That broker, that still breaks the pate of faith;
    That daily break-vow, he that wins of all,
    Of kings, of beggars, old men, young men, maids,—
    Who having no external thing to lose
    But the word "maid," cheats the poor maid of that;
    That smooth-faced gentleman, tickling Commodity,—
    Commodity, the bias of the world;
    The world, who of itself is peised well,
    Made to run even upon even ground,
    Till this advantage, this vile-drawing bias,

This sway on motion, this Commodity,
Makes it take head from all indifference,
From all direction, purpose, course, intent:
And this same bias, this Commodity,
This bawd, this broker, this all-changing word,
Clapt on the outward eye of fickle France,
Hath drawn him from his own determined aid,
From a resolved and honourable war,
To a most base and vile-concluded peace.—
And why rail I on this Commodity?
But for because he hath not woo'd me yet:
Not that I have the power to clutch my hand,
When his fair angels would salute my palm;
But for my hand, as unattempted yet,
Like a poor beggar, raileth on the rich.
Well, whiles I am a beggar, I will rail,
And say, There is no sin but to be rich:
And being rich, my virtue then shall be,
To say, There is no vice but beggary:
Since kings break faith upon commodity,
Gain, be my lord!—for I will worship thee!
(*Exit*)

OTHELLO

William Shakespeare

It is the end of the play. Othello has smothered Desdemona,
believing her to be unfaithful to him. When Emilia learns that
it was her husband, Iago, who told Othello that he thought that
Desdemona and Cassio were lovers, she denounces him as a liar

and explains that the fatal missing handkerchief which was instrumental in confirming Othello's suspicions had been given by her to Iago. Othello, realizing Iago's villainy, attacks him. Iago kills Emilia before escaping. The Moor is disarmed but, unknown to his captors still retains a weapon. Iago is brought back a prisoner, accompanied by Lodovico and Cassio. The former tells Othello

> "You must forsake this room and go with us.
>   Your power and your command is taken off,
> And Cassio rules in Cyprus."

Othello now makes his final speech. It would be superfluous to enlarge on the dramatic and tragic power of the verse here. The actor has to decide for himself the type and degree of characterization required. Widely different interpretations of this part have been given by some of our leading actors.

ACT V, SCENE ii

OTHELLO: Soft you; a word or two before you go.
    I have done the state some service, and they know't;—
    No more of that.—I pray you, in your letters,
    When you shall these unlucky deeds relate,
    Speak of me as I am; nothing extenuate,
    Nor set down aught in malice: then must you speak
    Of one that loved not wisely, but too well;
    Of one not easily jealous, but, being wrought,
    Perplext in the extreme; of one whose hand,
    Like the base Indian, threw a pearl away
    Richer than all his tribe; of one whose subdued eyes,
    Albeit unused to the melting mood,
    Drop tears as fast as the Arabian trees
    Their medicinable gum. Set you down this;
    And say besides, that in Aleppo once,
    Where a malignant and a turban'd Turk
    Beat a Venetian and traduced the state,
    I took by th'throat the circumcised dog,
    And smote him—thus. (*He stabs himself*)

LODOVICO: O bloody period!
GRATIANO: All that's spoke is marr'd.
OTHELLO: I kiss'd thee ere I kill'd thee: no way but this,
(*Falling upon* DESDEMONA)
Killing myself, to die upon a kiss. (*Dies*)

Omit Lodovico's and Gratiano's line.

THE WAKEFIELD MYSTERY PLAYS
edited by Martial Rose

Lazarus is one of the plays making up the Wakefield cycle of mystery plays which were performed in the mid-fifteenth century, probably in one fixed locality and on large decorated carts called pageants.

After Lazarus has been resurrected, Jesus orders that his bandages be removed from his hand, foot and throat. The stink of corrupted flesh at the opening of the tomb is emphasized in medieval literature and art.

After praising God, Lazarus goes on to describe the horrors of carnal corruption.

The speech has dramatic simplicity which, combined with medieval naïvety and the emotional content of the words, should make it an effective one.

LAZARUS: Lord, that all things made of nought,
    All praise be to thee,
    That such wonder here has wrought,
    Greater may none be.
    When I was dead hell's gate I sought,
    And thou, almighty,
    Raised me up and thence me brought,

172

Behold and ye may see.
There is none so bold decreed,
Nor none so proud to greet,
Nor none so doughty in his deed,

Nor none for dais more meet,
Nor king, nor knight, nor bondman freed,
Death's destiny could defeat,
Nor flesh where he was wont to feed,
But it shall be worms' meat.

Your death is worm's cook,
Your mirror here ye look,
And let me be your book,
    Example take from me;
Though charms for death ye took,
    Such shall ye all be.

Each one in such array, death shall him suddenly smite,
and close him in cold clay, whether he be king or knight
For all his garments gay that were a seemly sight,
His flesh shall fall away, as for many in this plight.
    On them a worm delights
    To gnaw at these gay knights,
    At their lungs and at their lights,
        Their hearts eaten asunder;
    These masters held the heights,
        Thus shall they be brought under.

Under the earth ye shall thus full of care then couch;
The roof of your hall your naked nose shall touch;
Neither great nor small to you will kneel nor crouch;
A sheet shall be your pall, toads for jewels will vouch;
    The slime of toads shall smear,
    The fiends fill you with fear,

Your flesh that fair was here
  Thus ruefully shall rot;
Instead of a gay collar
  Such bands shall bind your throat.

Your cheer that was so red, your looks the lily like,
Then shall be wan as lead and stink as dog in dyke;
And worms be in you bred as bees breed in a hive,
The eyes out of your head shall spotted toads thus rive;
  To pick you are pressed
  Many a loathsome beast,
  Thus they shall make a feast
    Of your flesh and of your blood.
  Your sorrows then are least
    When greatest seems your good.

Your goods ye shall forsake though ye be never so loth,
And nothing with you take but such a winding cloth;
Your wife's sorrow shall slake, also your children's both,
Your memory all shall forsake though ye be never so
wroth;
  They mind you as nothing
  That may be to your helping.
  Neither in mass singing
    Nor even with alms deed;
  Therefore in your leaving,
    Be wise and take good heed.

THE WHITE DEVIL
John Webster

John Webster based the play, which appeared in 1612, on the history of the Duke di Brachiano and his two wives, of whom Vittoria Corombona is the second. Flamineo is her brother.

The setting is Renaissance Italy, an apartment in Vittoria's house. Earlier in this scene there has been a suicide pact between the brother and sister, but Zanche, Vittoria's waiting-woman, has urged her mistress only to seem to consent to this, and to let Flamineo die first.

While they are together Ibdovico, Carlo, Casparo and Pedro enter and stab Vittoria, Flamineo and Zanche. Brother and sister defy their attackers, telling them that they have not stabbed deeply enough. During Flamineo's speech Vittoria dies. Webster was sometimes able to pack an infinity of agony and despair into a few simple, haunting phrases. He does so here.

ACT V, SCENE vi

FLAMINEO: Thou'rt a noble sister!
    I love thee now: if woman do breed man,
    She ought to teach him manhood: fare thee well.
    Know, many glorious women that are famed
    For masculine virtue have been vicious,
    Only a happier silence did betide them:
    She hath no faults who hath the art to hide them.
VITTORIA COROMBONA: My soul, like to a ship in a
    black storm,
    Is driven, I know not whither.
FLAMINEO: Then cast anchor.
    Prosperity doth betwitch men, seeming clear;
    But seas do laugh, show white, when rocks are near.
    We cease to grieve, cease to be fortune's slaves,
    Nay, cease to die, by dying. Art thou gone?
    And thou so near the bottom? false report,
    Which says that women vie with the nine Muses

For nine tough durable lives! I do not look
Who went before, nor who shall follow me;
No, at myself I will begin and end.
While we look up to Heaven, we confound
Knowledge with knowledge. Oh, I am in a mist!
VITTORIA COROMBONA: O, happy they that never saw
the court,
Nor ever knew great men but by report! (*Dies*)
FLAMINEO: I recover like a spent taper, for a flash,
And instantly go out.
Let all that belong to great men remember the old
wives' tradition, to be like the lions i' the Tower on
Candlemas-day: to mourn if the sun shine, for fear of
the pitiful remainder of winter to come.
'Tis well yet there's some goodness in my death;
My life was a black charnel. I have caught
An everlasting cold; I have lost my voice
Most irrecoverably. Farewell, glorious villains!
This busy trade of life appears most vain,
Since rest breeds rest, where all seek pain by pain.
Let no harsh flattering bells resound my knell;
Strike, thunder, and strike loud, to my farewell! (*Dies*)

Omit Vittoria Corombona's lines and Flamineo's "Then cast anchor."

INDEXES

INDEX OF AUTHORS

INDEX OF PLAYS

ACKNOWLEDGMENTS

Grateful acknowledgment is made to the following authors, agents, and publishers for permission to reproduce copyrighted material. No presentation of the speeches printed in this book may be given unless permission has first been obtained from the appropriate agents.

THE AFFAIR: Reprinted with the permission of Charles Scribner's Sons from *The Affair* by Ronald Millar from the novel by C. P. Snow. Copyright © 1962 Ronald Millar.

AH, WILDERNESS!: Copyright 1933 by Eugene O'Neill and renewed 1961 by Carlotta Monterey O'Neill. Reprinted from *The Plays of Eugene O'Neill*, by permission of Random House, Inc.

ALL GOD'S CHILLUN GOT WINGS: Copyright 1924 and renewed 1952 by Eugene O'Neill. Reprinted from *Nine Plays by Eugene O'Neill*, by permission of Random House, Inc.

AMERICA HURRAH!: Reprinted by permission of Coward, McCann & Geoghegan, Inc. from *America Hurrah!* by Jean-Claude van Itallie. Copyright © 1966, 1967 by Jean-Claude van Itallie.

THE AMERICAN DREAM: Reprinted by permission of Coward-McCann, Inc. from *The American Dream* by Edward Albee. Copyright © 1960, 1961 by Edward Albee.

ANDORRA: From *Andorra* by Max Frisch. Reproduced by permission of J. B. Lippincott Company.

THE ASCENT OF F6: From *The Ascent of F6*, by W. H. Auden and Christopher Isherwood. Copyright 1936, 1937 and renewed 1964 by W. H. Auden and Christopher Isherwood. Reprinted by permission of Random House, Inc.

THE BESPOKE OVERCOAT: Reproduced by permission of Curtis Brown Limited, London.

BILLY LIAR: Harvey Unna Limited.

BLUES FOR MISTER CHARLIE: Reprinted from *Blues for Mister Charlie* by James Baldwin. Copyright © 1964 by James Baldwin and used by permission of the publisher, The Dial Press, Inc.

THE BROWNING VERSION: Copyright, 1949, by Terence Rattigan. All Rights Reserved. CAUTION: *The Browning Version* is the sole property of the author and is fully protected by copyright. It may not be acted by professionals or amateurs without formal permission and the payment of a royalty. All rights, including professional, amateur, stock, radio and television, broadcasting, motion picture, recitation, lecturing, public reading, and the rights of translation into foreign languages are reserved. All inquiries should be addressed to the author's agent: Harold Freedman, Brandt & Brandt Dramatics Department, Inc., 101 Park Avenue, New York, N.Y. 10017.

187

188

rights of translation into foreign languages, are strictly reserved. Particular emphasis is laid on the question of readings, permission for which must be obtained in writing from the author's agents. All enquiries should be addressed to the author's agents: New Directions Publishing Corp., 333 Sixth Avenue, New York, N.Y. 10014.

THE ENTERTAINER: Reprinted by permission of S. G. Phillips, Inc., from *The Entertainer* by John Osborne. Copyright © 1958 by John Osborne.

EPITAPH FOR GEORGE DILLON: Reprinted by permission of S. G. Phillips, Inc., from *Epitaph For George Dillon* by John Osborne. Copyright © 1958 by John Osborne and Anthony Creighton.

THE FIRST BORN: From *The First Born* by Christopher Fry. © 1952, 1958 by Christopher Fry. Reprinted by permission of Oxford University Press, Inc.

GILT AND GINGERBREAD: Reproduced by permission of Curtis Brown Limited, London.

HADRIAN VII: From *Hadrian VII* by Peter Luke. Copyright © 1968 by Peter Luke. Reprinted by permission of Alfred A. Knopf, Inc.

THE HAMLET OF STEPNEY GREEN: Lom (Management) Limited.

THE HOLLY AND THE IVY: Reproduced by permission of Curtis Brown Limited, London.

I AM A CAMERA: From *I Am a Camera* by John Van Druten. Copyright 1952 by John Van Druten. Reprinted by permission of Random House, Inc.

ICARUS'S MOTHER: From *Five Plays*, copyright © 1967, by Sam Shepard, reprinted by permission of the publishers, The Bobbs-Merrill Company, Inc.

I'M TALKING ABOUT JERUSALEM: Theatrework (London) Limited.

THE IRREGULAR VERB TO LOVE: Evans Brothers Limited.

JUNO AND THE PAYCOCK: From *Juno and the Paycock* by Sean O'Casey. Reproduced by permission of St. Martin's Press, Inc., Macmillan & Co., Ltd., London.

KEEP TIGHTLY CLOSED IN A COOL DRY PLACE: Reproduced by permission of Megan Terry.

THE LARK: From *The Lark* by Jean Anouilh, translated by Christopher Fry. © 1955 by Christopher Fry. Reprinted by permission of Oxford University Press, Inc.

THE LESSON: Reprinted by permission of Grove Press, Inc. Copyright © 1958 by Grove Press, Inc.

THE LITTLE FOXES: From *The Little Foxes*, by Lillian Hellman. Reprinted by permission of Random House, Inc.

189

190

THE PROPOSAL: from Chekov: *Plays*, translated by Elisaveta Fen (Penguin Books).

THE PUBLIC EYE: Copyright © 1962 and 1964 by Peter Shaffer Ltd. From the book *The Private Ear, The Public Eye* by Peter Shaffer. Reprinted with permission of Stein and Day/Publishers.

PYGMALION: From *Pygmalion* by George Bernard Shaw. Reproduced by permission of The Society of Authors, London.

THE QUEEN AND THE REBELS: Translated by Henry Reed. Reprinted by permission of Grove Press, Inc. Copyright © 1956 by Andreina Betti.

A QUESTION OF FACT: Reproduced by permission of Curtis Brown Limited, London.

A RAISIN IN THE SUN: From *A Raisin in the Sun*, by Lorraine Hansberry. Copyright © 1958, 1959, 1966 by Robert Nemiroff as Executor of the Estate of Lorraine Hansberry. Reprinted by permission of Random House, Inc.

THE REHEARSAL: Reprinted by permission of Coward, McCann & Geoghegan, Inc., from *The Rehearsal* by Jean Anouilh, translated by Pamela Hansford Johnson and Kitty Black. Copyright © 1961 by Jean Anouilh, Pamela Hansford Johnson, and Kitty Black.

A RESOUNDING TINKLE: Reproduced by permission of Curtis Brown Limited, London.

RHINOCEROS: Reprinted by permission of Grove Press, Inc. Copyright © by John Calder (Publishers) Ltd. 1960.

ROBERT'S WIFE: Copyright 1938 by Macmillan Publishing Co., Inc. Reprinted from *Robert's Wife* by St. John Ervine by permission of Macmillan Publishing Co., Inc.

ROOTS: Theatrework (London) Limited.

ROSS: From *Ross*, by Terence Rattigan. Copyright © 1960 by Terence Rattigan. Reprinted by permission of Random House, Inc.

SOMETHING UNSPOKEN: Tennessee Williams, *27 Wagons Full of Cotton*. Copyright 1953 by Tennessee Williams. Reprinted by permission of New Directions Publishing Corporation. All rights reserved, including the right of reproduction in whole or in part in any form. CAUTION: Professionals and amateurs are hereby warned that *Something Unspoken*, being fully protected under the copyright laws of the United States, the British Empire including the Dominion of Canada, and all other countries of the Copyright Union, and other countries, is subject to royalty. All rights, including professional, amateur, motion-picture, recitation, lecturing, public reading, radio and television broadcasting, and the rights of translation into foreign languages, are strictly reserved. Particular emphasis is laid on the question of read-

191

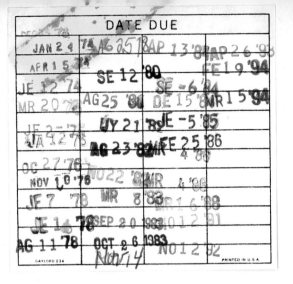